Overcoming the Trials of a Lifetime

Finding Meaning and Joy in the Midst of Afflictions, Illness, and Hardships

RANDALL K. BROBERG

WESTBOW
P R E S S®
A DIVISION OF THOMAS NELSON
& ZONDERVAN

WestBow Press books may be ordered through booksellers or by contacting:

WestBow Press
A Division of Thomas Nelson & Zondervan
1663 Liberty Drive
Bloomington, IN 47403
www.westbowpress.com
1 (866) 928-1240

Interior Image Credit: Randall K. Broberg

Scripture quotations are from the ESV® Bible (The Holy Bible, English
Standard Version®), copyright © 2001 by Crossway, a publishing ministry
of Good News Publishers. Used by permission. All rights reserved.

ISBN: 978-1-9736-6058-3 (sc)
ISBN: 978-1-9736-6059-0 (hc)
ISBN: 978-1-9736-6057-6 (e)

Library of Congress Control Number: 2019904808

Print information available on the last page.

WestBow Press rev. date: 5/13/2019

To my mother, Marilyn Totushek

She was, of course, responsible for my being here in the first place, but she also served as my copy editor and proofreader. She has my love and appreciation for all she's done in my life.

What Others Are Saying about
Overcoming the Trials of a Lifetime

Ray Bentley, author and founder/senior pastor of Maranatha Chapel, San Diego, California: This book is a testimony of overcoming that is so personal and powerful it will leave a deep impact on your soul. Randy Broberg's career as one of the top 100 intellectual property attorneys in California gives understanding to his brilliant and fresh insights into God's Word. On every level, it will leave you inspired and challenged. I can't wait for you to read it!

Dan Duncan, minister, Believers Chapel, Dallas, Texas: The world believes we have a right to be happy. In his book *Overcoming the Trials of a Lifetime*, Randall Broberg takes issue with that. God has promised His children something far better—joy in all circumstances, even the hardest ones. Randall's life is proof. His is a story of God's transforming grace through adversities and then chronic pain that produced spiritual growth, joy, and love for the Lord. More than an engaging narrative, the book is a scriptural analysis of affliction that challenges Christians to trust God through trials and be thankful. This book is an antidote for a generation hooked on being happy. I look forward to getting the book in the hands of people here. It's very good.

Dr. Gene A. Getz, professor, pastor, and author: I remember Randy Broberg well as a preteen, attending the church I pastored. He was inquisitive—and deeply interested in spiritual issues. Years later, he wandered in the wilderness of "unbelief"— but as a prodigal son. And when he "returned to the Father," he once again began to walk in God's path, demonstrating unusual faith blended with humility! This book tells his incredible journey. In spite of a life-altering illness, Randy is standing on the "solid rock" of faith in his Lord and Savior Jesus Christ.

Dr. Ron Jenson, author, speaker, America's Life Coach, San Diego, California: *Overcoming*—I *love* it—honest, thoughtful, funny, best handling of why we suffer I've read, great story, well written, and engaging.

Gary Lawton, senior pastor, Calvary Chapel, Santee, California: [*Overcoming*] is both wonderful and convicting. Randy reminded me that God is bigger than my circumstances, feelings, and failures. I know that though I don't see or understand what He allows in His personal plan for me, God is not fickle, mean, or simply proving some divine agenda. Randy's story and conclusions are sometimes hilarious and always insightful, interesting, and compelling. Overcoming will provide some much-needed medicine for folks.

Bruce B. Miller, senior pastor and author, Christ Fellowship, in McKinney, Texas: This is a gift that you will want to give to everyone you know who is suffering from a chronic condition. I intend to keep a stack on hand to give away. If you are in pain, this gift can bring you hope, and even joy.

Dr. Jim Newheiser, director of the Christian Counseling program, associate professor of counseling and practical theology, Reformed Theological Seminary, Charlotte: My friend Randy Broberg shares valuable practical lessons from scripture which are vividly illustrated by his unique life experiences.

Larry Osborn, pastor and author, North Coast Church, Vista, California: What do you say to someone burdened with broken dreams, deeply painful family memories, chronic pain or life-threatening illness? How do we help them find the joy and perspective that so quickly disappears in the dark valleys of life? In *Overcoming the Trials of a Lifetime*, Randy Broberg provides answers from the perspective of one who has lived in the valley. Diagnosed with young-onset Parkinson's disease, Randy's high-flying career as a technology lawyer, along with many of his plans and dreams, came to a screeching stop. Yet Randy learned firsthand that "the presence of real genuine pain doesn't negate the presence of real genuine joy." If you're in the valley (or know someone who is) and are struggling to experience God's presence in the valley, this is a book you need to read.

Through many dangers, toils, and snares,
  I have already come.
'Twas grace that brought me safe thus far.
  And grace will lead me home.
                    —John Newton, "Amazing Grace"

Contents

Foreword

It's a joy to receive a wrapped gift, especially one beautifully wrapped, and to tear open the paper and find inside something that makes your face break out in a huge smile.

This book, *Overcoming the Trials of a Lifetime*, is such a gift. It's a gift of rich insights wrapped in interesting stories from a man living in chronic pain, who is also a biblical scholar. Randy takes us into deeper understandings of faith, prayer, and healing.

For those who have lost hope in God, lost hope of ever feeling better—here is a gift from God. If you suffer from chronic pain or disability, this book offers you encouragement that just might restore your hope. If you are running from God, Randy understands. He ran too.

Randy says, "God wants us to have joy." And he gives insights that open our eyes to how we can find joy in the deepest trials, even trials that seem to have no end, at least in this life.

This gift comes from a man I know very well. Randy and I met in sixth grade. Through high school we were best of friends, challenging each other spiritually and intellectually. Then we went to different universities. In those days we wrote long letters to each other as dear friends. Slowly, I saw him drift away from God, until the sad day when I learned he had abandoned his faith.

For eighteen years, Randy wandered in the darkness. I remained his friend. He was a groomsman in my wedding, and I officiated his wedding. I prayed for him regularly. About every three months for all those years, I sent him a letter or an email, encouraging him to return to the Lord.

Then one Saturday afternoon, Randy called me. He told me that he had Parkinson's disease, which was tough to hear, but then he told me that he had returned to God! The prodigal had come home. I cried tears of joy. Since then, Randy has returned to ministry and is serving the Lord full time. We have ministered together. He has spoken at our church several times.

This gift you are looking at took decades to create. God crafted these messages into Randy's soul over many difficult and interesting experiences all over the world. It took a long time to wrap with years of stories, God-stories of adventures and tragedies.

This gift is carefully crafted by a biblical scholarship from a man who has had a first-rate education. Randy is one of the most intelligent people I know. His keen mind and tender heart come together to create this gift that will encourage you and inspire you and challenge you. Randy has a unique ability to make profound concepts simple and practical. Although he can communicate with the top scholars, he speaks in the language of everyday life for ordinary people.

This is a gift you will want to give to everyone you know who suffers from a chronic condition. I intend to keep a stack on hand to give away. If you are in pain, this gift can bring you hope and even joy.

When you unwrap this book and see what's inside, I believe your face will break out in a big smile as you realize that God is good and that you can once again have hope and joy, in spite of your circumstances.

Enjoy your gift!

Bruce B. Miller
Senior Pastor
Christ Fellowship, McKinney, Texas

Preface

My purpose in writing this book is to show you the discoveries I have made, discoveries of meaning and goodness and how you can be happy, even joyful, in the most extreme circumstances.

God is an author. In his unfathomable wisdom, he's written a story that are the stories of billions of his saints. Each story is individually moving and incredible in the natural sense and brings glory to God.

The apostle Paul's favorite method of sharing the gospel was by means of testimony. As you read the book of Acts, you will become acquainted with his testimony as he preached it to the Gentiles, as he defended himself in front of crowds of accusing Jews and on trial before the Romans. But he never gives us a complete autobiography. Indeed, the four Gospel accounts are not biographies either.

This book contains many stories from my life, but it is not the story of my life. That would require writing about the many relationships that matter, such as my relationship with my late father, my mother, my stepfather, my brothers, my wife, and my children. All these relationships have been and continue to be important and have shaped me or presently are shaping me. But these relationships are not the topic of this writing.

The story that follows includes my falling away and a prodigal period for eighteen years. It is my hope that because this story includes the prodigal's return, it will bring encouragement to parents and families that have experienced one or more of their children rejecting the faith as a young adult.

I also sincerely hope and believe my story and the scriptures taught in this book will benefit people who are in pain, have a chronic or life-threatening illness, are themselves or are the parents of physically or mentally challenged or sensory-impaired persons, or who are the caregivers of any of these.

Acknowledgments

I desire to recognize some of the support I have received. First among many is my mom, who guided me safely through a tumultuous childhood. Because he led me to Christ, I must thank and acknowledge my brother Karl. I suppose I'd still be wandering around if it weren't for him. I certainly must recognize my brother David for saving me from drowning. It's hard to compete with saving my soul or saving my body, but my brother Mark has always been there for me, and he was sort of a surrogate father for me when I was in my teens, teaching me how to drive not only a car but a motorcycle as well. My sophomore year in high school, I even lived in Mark's house.

As for recognizing gracious support in telling my story, the only possible choice is Ron Harper. Ron is my spiritual brother and one of my very few bests of friends. Simply put, without Ron's support, encouragement, and enthusiasm for this book project, this book would never have been written. And of course, I cannot forget the patience and understanding from my wife, Justine.

Chapter 1

The Pursuit of Happiness and Joy

Count it all joy, my brothers, when you meet trials
of various kinds, for you know that the testing of
your faith produces steadfastness. And let steadfastness have its full effect, that you may be perfect and complete, lacking in nothing.

—James 1:2–4

Happy Wives, Happy Lives

People today have become convinced that their own personal
happiness is the be all and end all—that it is the most important thing.

We live in a country that promises us an "inalienable right"
to the "pursuit of happiness." You know the problem starts with
what the world promises. We think we have a guaranteed, unde-
niable right to be happy. We believe it's a right in the Declaration
of Independence.

People are given counsel like this: "You can't help other people until you find your own happiness. Then, after you've found
your own happiness, you can share it with others."

Heard that before? Or how about this one: "The only important thing is how you feel about yourself." That's not the only
important thing, is it?

According to modern dictionaries, *joy* is the emotion evoked by well-being, success, or good fortune or by the prospect of possessing what one desires. The world defines *happy* as the feeling experienced when one's wishes are met. Interestingly, the world says that joy is happiness and that they are synonyms.

The world's understanding of happiness and joy is that you have it when you get what you want. When you get what you want, you're happy, and if you're not getting what you want, you're unhappy. It's like we've all grown up into these big adult bodies, but we're still just a bunch of toddlers.

If you start off with that kind of definition, you'll go nowhere really fast. Based on the world's definition, this is what people will sound like:

> "I'll be happy when I buy that new car."
> "I'll be happy when I get that promotion."
> "I'll be happy if we can have another child."
> "I'll be happy if we never have more children."

This getting whatever we desire isn't going to happen, so if we are rational at all, we will curb our expectations. My parents taught me about the defense mechanism—if we want something badly, we won't get it, and so we need to lower our expectations to avoid disappointment.

If our circumstances determine whether we will have joy, we will be very disappointed. Joy isn't going to happen for us. We Christians have the same set of circumstances as non-Christians do. Even if we get what we want, we could lose it the next day. It's easy to see the world is setting us up for frustration and disappointment. It promises us happiness based on our getting what we want.

These two views of joy and happiness are just messed up. These definitions apply to screaming toddlers who don't get their way, not to people, saved or not, who have even an inkling of how to live in a world where they seldom get their way or where they can even lose the things and people they held most dear.

God's kingdom is all about righteousness, peace, and joy and *not* about escaping earthly suffering or acquiring everything we want.

Happy or Joyful in the Bible

The word *happy* is not usually in our Bible translations. The Bible uses the word *joy*. *Joy* substitutes for *happiness* but is not a synonym, meaning these two words are not interchangeable. For our purposes, we'll just run with the word joy rather than the word happiness.

The words *joy, rejoice,* and *enjoy* are all basically the same word in both Greek and English. *Joy* is the noun, while *rejoice* and *enjoy* are the verbs. *Joyful* and *joyfully* are the adjective and adverb, respectfully.

In the Old Testament, joy was connected mostly to shouting and singing. Accordingly, the greatest number of Old Testament uses of joy are in connection with shouting and singing, as in shout and sing joyfully.

In the New Testament, I separated each verse (without ignoring context) into different categories. The results were easy to ascertain because there is little ambiguity. These verses act as promises of God, and his faithfulness depends on the truth of them in our lives.

Because of the way the word is used in the Bible, you can infer that this kind of joy is visible and audible (e.g., shouting, singing) The biblical word *joy* does not sound like, "Oh yes, son, I'm very joyful today." No, it's like you're in a tavern where everybody's watching the playoff game on the big screen, and then your home team scores a touchdown, and you jump, shouting, "High five!" That's joy. You'll know it when you feel it.

Next, I reviewed every verse in the Bible that referenced joy, rejoice, enjoy, or joyful. I then asked, Who is joyful. and why are they joyful?

As I began reading and studying what the Bible says about joy, I was blown away by my first three observations.

God Wants You to Be Joyful

The first principle I learned from that study was that God wants you to have joy in your life. On more than one occasion,[1] Jesus said the purpose of the words he had spoken was to bring full and complete joy to his disciples. Disciples? That means you and me.

I would think that if Jesus was on your side, and you wanted happiness, then there's a good chance you can have it if you ask for it.[2]

Then he says he's going to give you what you ask of him, according to his will. He just said he wants you to be happy. That's his will. Does he say that you will get everything you want, and your happiness will come from that? No. That's the world's definition.

The apostle John makes the same points in 1 John 1:4, where he says, "We are writing these things so that our joy may be complete. You will be sorrowful, but your sorrow will turn into joy." First John 1:4 says that God wants you to have complete joy. The writings John had in mind are in the Bible.

Paul prays for us in Romans 15:13, saying, "May the God of hope fill you with all joy." He wants us to have real joy. Remember that Jesus spoke and John wrote so that your joy would be full.

Therefore, when you are suffering or in pain, when you have experienced a financial setback, or when your marriage or family is in jeopardy, turn to the Word of God for comfort amid your afflictions; turn for comfort for your soul, found in the Bible, especially the psalms.

True Joy Comes from God, not Circumstances

The second principle was that joy has nothing to do with your circumstances and everything to do with your relationship with God.

---

[1] See, e.g., John 15:11 and 16:24.
[2] See, for example, Romans 14:16–17.

Note how Paul describes his circumstances in 2 Corinthians 7:4–5:

> I am acting with great boldness toward you; I have great pride in you; I am filled with comfort. In all our affliction, I am overflowing with joy. For even when we came into Macedonia, our bodies had no rest, but we were afflicted at every turn—fighting without and fear within.

And again he writes in 2 Corinthians 8:1–2:

> We want you to know, brothers, about the grace of God that has been given among the churches of Macedonia, for in a severe test of affliction, their abundance of joy and their extreme poverty have overflowed in a wealth of generosity on their part.

Some of you already know this principle intuitively because you have seen people who have no pain yet seem to be devoid of joy. Even people who have all beneficial circumstances lined up like ducks in a row can whine and complain and generally see the dark side of every cloud.

You Can Be Joyful in Your Trial or Suffering

The third principle was that joy can come to you while you are right in the middle of a trial. In other words, joy and pain can be felt at the same time. The presence of genuine pain does not negate the presence of genuine joy. Here it is clear: one can have joy during the affliction or trial, not just after the suffering is past.

Paul prays for us:

> The presence of genuine pain does not negate the presence of genuine joy. Here it is clear: one can have joy during the affliction or trial, not just after the suffering is past.

5

And so, from the day we heard, we have not ceased to pray for you, asking that you may be filled with the knowledge of his will in all spiritual wisdom and understanding, so as to walk in a manner worthy of the Lord, fully pleasing to him, bearing fruit in every good work and increasing in the knowledge of God. May you be strengthened with all power, according to his glorious might, for all endurance and patience with joy, giving thanks to the Father, who has qualified you to share in the inheritance of the saints in light. (Colossians 1:9–12)

Paul is asking for us to have power so that we may have endurance and patience. Do you think he's talking about going through a trial? Sounds to me like he's talking about a trial. But Paul is not praying for us only to get through the trial. He is praying that we'll be joyful during and amid the trial. That's a whole other ball game. He doesn't just want us to survive the trial; he wants us to be joyful *in* the trial.

Peter makes the same point:

In this you rejoice, though now for a little while, if necessary, you have been grieved by various trials, so that the tested genuineness of your faith—more precious than gold that perishes though it is tested by fire—may be found to result in praise and glory and honor at the revelation of Jesus Christ. Though you have not seen him, you love him. Though you do not now see him, you believe in him and rejoice with joy that is inexpressible and filled with glory. (1 Peter 1:6–8)

In 1 Thessalonians 1:6, Paul writes, "And you became imitators of us and of the Lord, for you received the word in much affliction, with the joy of the Holy Spirit." John also speaks of the same principle of joy arising out of affliction in John 16:20: "Truly, truly, I say to you, you will weep and lament, but the world will rejoice. You will be sorrowful, but your sorrow will turn into joy."[3]

God is nice; he is not mean. He's not making you go through those trials to hurt you. God is promising you that his purpose is for you to have full joy, even in this life. True joy comes from God, even when the circumstances are unfavorable, harsh, harmful, or just plain bad.

> God is not saying you won't have your property plundered. He's saying even if your property is plundered, you still can be joyful. He's praying that you'll be joyful in your trial. He isn't praying for the trial to end.

About financial setbacks, Hebrews 10:34 says, "For you had compassion on those in the prison and you joyfully accepted the plundering of your property since you knew that you yourselves had a better possession and an abiding one." That's amazing. It's crucial to understand that the Hebrews had their joy in abundance and overflowing while experiencing extreme poverty; their joy came while they were in poverty, not because their poverty had ended. In fact, Hebrews 10:34 makes it clear they were getting poorer when they had joy.

God is not saying you won't have your property plundered. He's saying even if your property is plundered, you still can be joyful. He's praying that you'll be joyful in your trial. He isn't praying for the trial to end.

Something unexpected is going on here, and it's because affliction is real. The people really lost their jobs. The person really got sick. The loved one really did die. Those are real things that hurt. The trial stinks, and it's very real. Your affliction is *real*.

Joy comes despite and without respect to the circumstances, but the joy is just as real as the affliction. And it is from God.

---

[3] See 1 John 1:4; also John 17:13.

Count It All as Joy

Here is the Word of God, written to us by James, the brother of our Lord: "Count it all joy, my brothers, when you meet trials of various kinds" (James 1:2). A likely reaction:

Oh yeah, sure. I'm going to go through this trial. I'm going to suffer. Someone I love is going to suffer, and I'm going to count it as joy, say that's joy, and reckon it a joy (I'm from Texas). I'll even wear a smile to hide my anger or disappointment.

At first glance, James seems to imply we can just wave a magic wand and turn the trial into joy. Notice very carefully, though, that James is not telling us we will count it as joy when we get our job or retirement fund back. He is not waiting to count it as joy when the sick are healed. He means we need to count it as joy while we still hurt and before God restores us or heals us.

When you lost your job, you really lost your job. Counting it as joy doesn't give you your job back. When your retirement was based on the home equity in Southern California, and then home equity went poof, counting it as joy doesn't raise your appraisal. If your 401(k) just disappeared, counting it joy won't put that retirement plan back in place either.

But no matter how incurable or painful, when a godly perspective is maintained, one can see that in every case, the trial is no comparison to what God has in store. See the eternal—even heavenly—perspective written by the apostle Peter in 1 Peter 1:3–9.[4] What gives us joy when we are in affliction is our faith and hope in our Lord Jesus Christ.

The problem I saw was that we may count it as joy, but the trial might not go away.

How can we understand going through a trial or tribulation, being afflicted and suffering, and still be joyful? It is difficult, but I think we can grasp the basic truth: if we have faith that God is

---

[4] See also Luke 6:22–23.

nice and not mean and that he has a fantastic plan for our lives that is beyond our comprehension, then we should understand that for some good to be achieved in our lives, we might need to endure painful afflictions.

NOTES

Chapter 2

The Wander Years

The heart of man plans his way, but the Lord es-
tablishes his steps.

—Proverbs 26:9

Some wandered in desert wastes, finding no way
to a city to dwell in; hungry and thirsty, their soul
fainted within them.

Then they cried to the Lord in their trouble,
and he delivered them from their distress. He led
them by a straight way till they reached a city to
dwell in. Let them thank the Lord for his steadfast
love for his wondrous works to the children of
man. For he satisfies the longing soul, and the
hungry soul he fills with a good thing.

—Psalm 107:4–9

I was born in Minneapolis, Minnesota, at the Swedish Hospital
on a cold and snowy night in February 1961.

Memories that Shaped Me

Although I was baptized as an infant in the Lutheran Church,
during my early childhood my only contact with Christ,
Christianity, or the church was through my grandmother (my

father's mother), who taught me simple childhood prayers, gave me my first Bible, and was an avid listener of Billy Graham's radio program. My grandmother also took me to Lutheran church camp in the summer, somewhere in northern Minnesota, but all I remember from that experience was swimming and waiting in long lines for meals. I have no memories of attending church, Sunday school, or anything religious in my early life, beyond saying grace before meals.

As most would measure it, my early childhood in Minnesota was traumatic.

My father was a US Marine and a first responder/fireman who saved lives from burning buildings. It was a very stressful job. At some point during those years, my dad's mental health began to deteriorate. When I was about seven years old, my father had what used to be called a nervous breakdown and was placed in a psychiatric hospital. One of my earliest Christmas memories is of visiting my father at a Veterans' Hospital and seeing him in the lobby, dressed in a bathrobe and smoking a cigarette while nervously looking over his shoulder repeatedly.

> My most enduring memory from those days is of sitting at the top of the stairs, weeping, as I watched my dad hauled away in an ambulance, wearing a straight-jacket.

They said my dad had paranoid schizophrenia. I don't know if that diagnosis was correct. The only treatment he was offered was a good night's sleep in a padded and windowless room, along with a tranquilizer or two to help the time pass. Sounds kind of medieval to me.

My most enduring memory from those days is of sitting at the top of the stairs, weeping, as I watched my dad hauled away in an ambulance, wearing a straight-jacket.

Wander in the Woods

When I was five or six years old, my family went on a camping vacation in a national park. The campsite was very interesting to me. I was particularly impressed with the long, large culvert that spanned the road above—sort of a magical tunnel.

Beyond the culvert was a parking lot with several rows of cars, and it was connected to the campsite area only by the culvert. Our family had a pickup truck parked in the lot and a camper trailer parked at the campsite.

My three older brothers decided we kids should go for a hike to explore the park, leaving our mom and dad at the campsite. I was five years younger than my nearest-in-age brother, so I was on the tail end of the hike. I tried hard to keep up, but I soon became tired of the hike.

I asked my brothers to take it a little bit easier and give me a chance to rest, but my pleas were unheeded. So I decided to take my own rest and return the way we'd come. The trek through the woods in the opposite direction from my brother's path didn't seem difficult. There were trails to follow and even the occasional sign, although, at age five, I couldn't read the signs. I didn't know if my brothers had turned back or even if they had noticed I was no longer with them.

It was already late in the day when I came upon a parking lot. I thought I'd soon be back with Mom and Dad and in time for supper, but the trouble was, it was the wrong parking lot.

There was no family pickup, no culvert, and no parents cooking dinner. What was I to do? I wasn't going to give up so easily, so I climbed an embankment to get a good look around. Spanning the horizon, I noticed another campsite in the distance. Could that be our campsite, the one with the culvert? I was getting hungry, so I determined I should make a beeline directly to the camp I'd spotted. The sun was setting, but it wouldn't be dark immediately, so I was sure I could make it.

You probably can figure out what happened. Soon afterward,

I was lost in a forest in the dark. Like many who had been lost in the forest, I found myself going in circles. I might not have realized I was going in circles until I was told later, but it was clear I was alone in the forest—and apparently, the entire campground was searching the woods for me.

My mom must have had many scenarios going through her head: *Could he have been snatched? Could there be a bear? Is he just lost out there in the dark forest?*

Then I remembered what my dad, the Boy Scout, had told my brothers and me—"If you ever get lost and it's a dark night, let the North Star guide you." He said that the North Star always maintained a position that was due north, so it could be followed. This would prevent us from walking in circles, even if the destination was not north. Thankfully, my dad had also shown me how to find the North Star (it had to do with the stars of the Big and Little Dippers, as I recall). I followed the North Star and soon found a dirt road, which I then followed until I was picked up by park rangers and returned to my family—still in time for dinner. My brothers were severely disciplined by our dad.

My Thoughts and Views

In retrospect, I'm not sure the angles of the stars and the North Star indicating north would have been much help to me in the small space of the forest where I had gone missing. I don't remember being afraid, but I wasn't missing very long—not long enough to be famous, like that girl who fell into a well or even like Tom Sawyer getting lost in the cave.

But does it matter? I believe God refreshed my memory about the North Star, which resulted in my believing I was being guided by the star. And so believing, I walked in a straight line until I met the road. It didn't need to be complicated. God wasn't done with me yet.

I Am the Wanderer

When I was about six years old, I got lost leaving my home in Minneapolis to go the Saint Paul Zoo, located across the Mississippi River many miles to the east.

I liked going to the zoo because I loved animals. In fact, I had formed a club of neighborhood children called the Animal Lovers Club. One of the charter members of the club was Daniel, a five-year-old who lived next door. You might guess what happened. I persuaded Daniel that I knew how to get to the zoo, and we immediately embarked on the journey to Saint Paul.

Our house was on a street that led straight to a city park and around a lake called Lake of the Isles. The lake was about twenty blocks from my house. The street and Lake of the Isles were north/south; the way to the Saint Paul Zoo was east/west. I didn't know that.

Fortunately, when we got to the lake, we were already too tired to walk any farther, so we headed back. The problem was, we took a different street when we started back and soon found ourselves off course.

Meanwhile, my parents realized we were missing, and a battalion of police and firemen who knew my dad were searching everywhere for little Randy and Daniel. From their point of view, our being snatched was the most likely and most feared scenario.

On our return trip, Daniel and I actually passed the street where I lived but didn't know it. Finally, we came up to Whittier Elementary School, where my older brothers had attended. Once I recognized the school, I knew the way home—to the left until we got to the A&W Root Beer, and then down to the church on the corner, and then one block to the right, and then we were safe and sound.

Home Alone

My dad and his family were all outdoorsmen. Every year we kids would load ourselves into the camper on the back of my dad's pickup truck; Mom and Dad would ride in the cab. Sometimes I got to ride in the front, and sometimes I was put in the back with my brothers. There was no direct way to communicate between the camper on the back and the cab of the truck.

One time we were getting ready to go camping, and I was playing in the dirt in front of the house because my dad had just watered the plants. It was like a little tiny flood that I enjoyed while pretending I was a little god in charge of that place.

I was so engrossed that I paid no attention to getting in the camper. I didn't heed the call to get in the truck when it was time to go; I was too focused on what I was doing in the dirt. When I looked around for the truck, it was gone. I ran past the next-door neighbor's house on the street corner and saw the truck off in the distance, heading away.

I held back my tears as I ran, block after block, trying to chase down my dad's truck. Finally, they came to a long stop-light, and I was able to catch up to them. You should've seen the look on my mother's face when she saw her son running up on the sidewalk, next to her in the cab of the truck. Apparently, the boys in the back thought I was riding in the cab with our parents, and our parents thought I was riding in the back with the boys. I guess it was my own version of the *Home Alone* experience.

I Almost Drowned—Twice

I nearly drowned on two occasions.

The first time was at my uncle's lake house. One summer evening, I went down to the dock outside my uncle's cabin when everyone else was inside. I was bending over, looking into the water, and I fell into the lake in water over my head. I was only about six or seven years old and didn't know how to swim.

I remember very distinctly looking up while swallowing water and seeing the sun and green light underneath the lake surface as I sank down and struggled against it. Thankfully, my brother David, who was eleven or twelve, was looking out the window of the cabin and saw me fall off the dock. Without talking to anybody or calling to Mom or Dad, he went high-tailing it right through the front door, out to the dock, and into the water and saved me.

God wasn't done with me yet.

The second time was when I was about eight years old. I was on vacation at a dude ranch with a group of other children. The camp counselors took us to a creek to swim. As I was swimming, an undercurrent pulled me under the water to the point where I could no longer see the surface.

Normally, I would have struggled to reach the surface, but something told me that I shouldn't do that. Maybe it was the memory of falling off the dock at my uncle's cabin. My head told me to swim sideways below the water, not straight up. So I swam under the water, holding my breath, and very soon I was in the shallow water of the creek bank. I couldn't see through the murky water, but I felt the dirt of the bottom hitting my chest. I knew then that I was safe.

I don't know what gave me the presence of mind to think logically when I was pulled underwater, but I did. God wasn't done with me yet.

My Father's Mental Illness.

Somewhere around 1967 or '68, something snapped for my dad. My dad was in and out of the Veterans' Hospital, and during one of the times when he was home, I experienced one of the saddest and most frightening events of my life.

My father feared he would lose my mom to divorce. Acting upon this fear, he abandoned reason and held my mom against her will in a bathroom in the house. He threatened to kill her, but after several hours, my mom talked her way out.

The following week, he grabbed me and took me to his bedroom. But this time was different from his keeping Mom in the bathroom. Dad didn't

> After locking the door, he retrieved his favorite handgun from the closet, a World War II German Lugar.

threaten me or hurt me, but he did force me to take two sleeping pills, and then he told me to calm down and be quiet. After locking the door, he retrieved his favorite handgun from the closet, a World War II German Lugar.

Soon, the police were on the other side of the door, demanding that he give me up and saying, "Come out with your hands where we can see them." Very quickly, the police had ascertained that my father was a veteran and a firefighter with the Minneapolis Fire Department. This afforded my dad some time to think, as the police agreed to stand down out of professional courtesy to a fellow first responder.

Soon after that, my uncle Bob, Dad's brother and also a Minneapolis fireman, arrived and talked through the door with my dad. Bob eventually removed the bolts from the door and convinced my dad to surrender.

Gone to Texas

Not surprisingly, my parents were separated soon afterward when my mom and I moved out for safety reasons. I was eight years old.

A year later—it was 1970—my parents divorced, and my mother married Tom. We moved to Dallas, Texas, as a way to escape the situation.

I didn't hear from or see my brothers for several years because while I was in Texas, they remained in Minnesota.

During this period, my dad traveled the country and sent me postcards made from actual photos of him carrying a Machete knife and wearing a cowboy hat and bandana or wearing a suit with sunglasses on while standing in a casino. I received cards and letters from places like Panama, Las Vegas, and New Orleans, almost always with a cryptic message—things like, "Here's my friend Herbert Hoover [sic], the FBI director, and I've been talking to him about how you were kidnapped, and he's going to have the FBI investigate it." This was crazy stuff, but again, there wasn't really any medicine he could take that was better than just being tranquilized.

For the next several years, my only contact with my father was through the postcards and letters he sent as he wandered aimlessly around the country. I feared my father and was on the lookout for him. I took precautions against being kidnapped.

NOTES

Chapter 3

Zealous Youth

And I am sure of this, that he who began a good work in you will bring it to completion at the day of Jesus Christ.

—Philippians 1:6

Salvation

I was born again at home in Dallas, Texas, sometime in 1973. I was twelve years old.

My brother Karl had found Christ while in high school and was visiting us while on leave from the army during the very end of the Vietnam War. He explained to me that I was a sinner in need of God's mercy and that Christ had died for me and would save me from my sins and eternal punishment if only I'd believe and place my trust in him. God had readied my heart to listen and understand this simple witness, but I didn't immediately accept Christ.

After several discussions with my brother, I remember being alone in the house when I got down on my knees in the hallway right outside my bedroom door, and I prayed to God, asking him to forgive me for my sins and to save me.

My Thoughts and Views

Salvation in the New Testament is not merely about that one day in the past when you were "saved." It's about *being saved* continually throughout your life. It's about waiting and trusting that upon your death, you will be truly and finally saved from sin—saved not just from the penalty of sin but from its power over you.

Baby Christian.

Karl gave me a copy of the New Testament in the "Good News for Modern Man" translation, and I devoured it like a starving person at a dinner table. Karl also gave me several comic book descriptions of the Christian life—how I should walk and grow in the Christian life. God's Holy Spirit motivated me to try to grow fast in the Christian faith.

After I'd devoured the Good News New Testament, Karl gave me his own copy of the Scofield Reference Bible, and he encouraged me to read ten chapters per day. I, however, thought the Bible was a book, so I read it front to back, as I would have read any other book.

Father's Suicide

In 1975, I met my father again for the first time in five years; as it turned out, it was for the last time. My brother Mark escorted me to a restaurant, where I could meet Dad safely in a public place. I hardly knew the man and still feared him.

When we met again, I was somewhat shocked by his behavior and attitude—he was flirting with the young waitress. I prayed one of the only prayers I truly regretted praying later—that God would somehow teach him a lesson. I regretted that prayer because about three months later on my mother's birthday—July 21, 1975—we received a telephone call from my uncle Bob, who told us that my father had committed suicide that day by a gunshot to the head.

My dad's death and the funeral trip to Minnesota was a real test of my newfound faith. I was fourteen years old.

After my father's death, I faced increasing struggles at home in my relationship with my stepfather; I had a very poor relationship with him. Part of this was that I was going through my teenage years. Another part of it was the classic stepparent dynamic. I needed help and counseling to get through it, and this caused me to turn increasingly toward the church and to rely on God.

My Calling

I was disillusioned with the Lutheran church I'd been attending. One day I was walking down Arapaho Road in Dallas headed toward the Piggly Wiggly grocery store when I walked past a sign on the road in front of a very small house-like building that said, "Fellowship Bible Church." I felt that this was some sort of divine sign for me because fellowship and Bible were exactly what I lacked and what I longed for.

Fellowship Bible Church became my church in every way. I shared during the sharing service; I taught small children in the Sunday School; I got involved with the high school group, and I participated in mini-churches (Fellowship's version of a home fellowship). I was mentored and discipled by some of the pastors there and by some Dallas Theological Seminary students. I also got to know Gene Getz, the pastor, very well and read all his books.

I also attended Believers Chapel in Dallas when the primary teaching elder was S. Lewis Johnson Jr. These two men, Getz and Johnson, taught me so much that even today, more than thirty years later, I turn to their teaching.

> One Sunday evening, I stood up in front of the congregation and preached for about fifteen minutes.

Believers Chapel is a church that allows the free exercise of gifts during a spontaneous Sunday evening Lord's Supper service. At this service, any member of the congregation is free to stand up and share, exhort, sing, or teach, as the Spirit so moves. It was at these services that I first began to preach.

One Sunday evening, I stood up in front of the congregation and preached for about fifteen minutes from my notes about what God meant to me as a Father, in light of my not having a human father. My primary text was taken from a Simon and Garfunkel song, which I quoted extensively. The "sermon" was well received by the congregation, and several of the elders encouraged me to speak again.

One time I was preaching about the importance of a Christian education. I guess I went on too long, as before I was finished, another member of the congregation arose and said, "While Brother Randy finishes, let's all stand and sing a hymn"—and he mentioned a hymn number.

I was quite shocked but more shocked when Dr. Johnson immediately stood and said, "No, let him finish." What an experience.

I believed the congregation and elders of Believers Chapel recognized that I had a gift, and the elders encouraged me to consider the ministry as my vocational calling. I too was convinced that I would go into the ministry and that this was my true calling.

NOTES

Chapter 4

Deliberate Disobedience

How can a young man keep his way pure? By guarding it according to your word. With my whole heart I seek you; let me not wander from your commandments! I have stored up your word in my heart, that I might not sin against you.

—Psalm 119:9–11

Remember not the sins of my youth or my transgressions; according to your steadfast love remember me, for the sake of your goodness, O Lord!

—Psalm 25:7

College Days

I began my studies at Stanford University in the fall of 1979. I was eighteen years old.

That first year at Stanford was exciting and life-changing. I was constantly surrounded by teachers and students who were brilliant. There was the premed surfer from Orange County, California. There was the space-camp summer scientist, majoring in physics. There was the Hawaiian dancer girl who grew up in rural Hawaii on the "Big Island" and whose parents were missionaries there. Thinking that my friends and teachers were brilliant caused self-doubt; it was only natural to ask myself, "What am I doing here with these people?"

I was in a veritable cafeteria of learning experiences, with no limits. I think heaven will be something like attending Stanford, except for the political and politically correct stuff.

> My personal prayer and Bible-study habits first wavered and then withered

Meanwhile, my personal prayer and Bible-study habits first wavered and then withered. My efforts to continue in personal fellowship with Christ began to fail. I didn't have a car, so I was unable to drive myself to church; I relied on the occasional chance to ride with someone else to the driver's church. In this way, I visited Menlo Park Presbyterian Church and Peninsula Bible Church (where Ray Stedman[5] was), but because of transportation difficulties, I was unable to become very active in either. Although I'd attended church several times a week in high school, I now found myself doing well to attend church once a month.

I did get involved in InterVarsity Christian Fellowship and a small organization on campus called the Christian Studies Association (which made me its president). I attended and led on-campus Bible studies, attempted to witness to my dorm mates, and went on retreats.

Outside of the Christian groups, however, such activities did not win me a lot of friends on campus. I began to feel lonely. I lived in dormitories surrounded by non-Christians, and I wanted to have more friends, to be more "normal" and not such an outsider.

As a sign of things to come, I was asked to be the leader of the InterVarsity chapter at Stanford, but I turned it down because

---

[5] Ray Stedman was a nationally known pastor on the cutting edge of the 1970s evangelical transformation of Sunday church through his bestselling book, "Body Life."
.Gene A Getz was also a leader of that church reform movement through his book, "Sharpening the Focus of the Church."

I was concerned that the time commitment would adversely affect my grade point average.

My Thoughts and Theories

My being far from home, unaccountable to a church or even my family, and surrounded by temptations of the flesh I'd never experienced until that time, I began a seemingly endless cycle of sin, guilt, and repentance, followed by growth, followed by sin again. A big part of my turning my back on God's calling for my life was guilt; an even larger part was that I was just plain tired, exhausted, and ready to quit; I felt defeated. I'd hoped God would have used me to lead a nation like Joseph or lead a great reformation of the church like John Calvin or preach like Charles Spurgeon, but I was a spiritual failure.

Perhaps if I had returned to any good church where I could have reconnected with fellow believers, I might have returned to God sooner. But I was cut off and far away from my Christian friends and mentors. And no one held me accountable,

> I began a seemingly endless cycle of sin, guilt, and repentance, followed by growth, followed by sin again.

rebuked me, or disciplined me. Accordingly, I strayed further away during the following years, and, as a result, my heart got harder and harder.

If it came to defending the faith, arguing evolution versus creation, or any number of other things, I was thoroughly and adequately prepared. No professor or seminar class was my undoing. On the contrary, in classrooms, I regularly defended my faith, and I felt no fear of the non-Christian intellectual academic citadel.

You can prepare your children to face attacks from non-Christian worldviews, but if they're not prepared to deal with sin, there's going to be a problem. Sooner or later, they will sin, but how will they deal with the consequences and the aftermath of sin?

I should have known better. God relates to his children as their Father, not as their judge.

Athens, Greece

It was in this context of withering church attendance, Bible study, and prayer that I ventured off to Europe in the summer of 1981 to study archaeology and ancient history in Athens and Rome. I went to Greece without a Bible or prayer. There was no church to attend and no fellow believers to hold me accountable. I was alone.

At the American School of Classical Studies in Athens, I spent the entire summer in close quarters with a woman colleague who

> I told myself that I was quitting—getting off the bus, as it were—and resigned myself to a life of failure, spiritually.

encouraged my lust and desires. At first, I was somewhat like Joseph running away from Potiphar's wife, but eventually, my resistance was worn down. One day, while riding a bus, I weighed the balance between my flesh and my spirit, and my flesh prevailed. I walked away from the ministry and even my relationship with Christ. I told myself that I was quitting—getting off the bus, as it were—and resigned myself to a life of failure, spiritually.

I weighed my life and future. On one hand, I saw a life in the ministry but one I thought would be characterized by moral defeat, endless guilt, failure, and—most likely—hypocrisy. On the other hand, I saw surrender to the lusts of the flesh and a future being nothing more than a mere back-pew Christian. When I chose the latter, a perceived weight dropped from my shoulders. Removed was the burden associated with such high expectations.

Sadly, rather than repenting, I convinced myself (or perhaps the devil convinced me) that I was no longer worthy to serve God and that my life could no longer honor him. After giving in to temptation, I felt so guilty and alienated and isolated from God that my heart broke and then hardened and scarred. I felt unworthy to serve in God's ministry. My witness had been lost. My testimony had been destroyed; my moral authority decimated.

Something inside me didn't want to bring Christ to shame, however, so I resolved to deny Christ; that is, to deny to people that I was a Christian so that my behavior would not tarnish his name. But I also determined that thereafter, I would no longer deal with the guilt associated with repentance. I felt as though I'd gone through a portal and was now on the other side with the sinners.

Since I clearly could not remain holy, even with all the advantages God had provided me, I believed I didn't deserve to go to heaven (but Satan was deceiving me as to the solution).

Perhaps I'd still go to heaven, but there'd be no ministry for me, the hypocrite. I felt a lot like Adam likely felt when he hid from the Lord in the garden of Eden, wearing leaves for clothing to cover his shame. I was also like the Prodigal, in that I felt that I had asked for my inheritance and was then going to spend it.

NOTES

Chapter 5

Prodigal Period

I have gone astray like a lost sheep.
                    —Psalm 119:176

Dead Sea Scrolls Expedition

After my time in Greece, I went to Israel and had a few adventures with my traveling companion, Todd. The two most notable adventures were in the desert at the Qumran Caves and in Jerusalem at Hezekiah's Tunnel.

Todd and I hired a taxi to take us to the Dead Sea. We went to a fancy rest-stop kind of place by the Dead Sea, where you can see the Qumran Caves, where the Dead Sea Scrolls were discovered in 1947–48. You can identify the caves if you stand in a certain place and look through a window. They were only about half a mile from where we were standing. We began to wonder and tempt ourselves: *"Maybe there are more Dead Sea Scrolls out there to be found. Why not?"*

This was 1981 and not surprisingly, there was no security and no guards or even a fence. As a couple of amateur archaeologists from California, we knew we would never again be so close to these caves, so we immediately proceeded to the cave cliffs and began the ascent. This was the beginning of our expedition. Soon, I went into one of the caves—no flashlight, no ropes, no first-aid kit. (What was I thinking?)

When I was in the desert sun, my eyes were dilated, and I was squinting because the sun was so very bright. So when I went into the cave that was as dark as dark could be, I stood there so that my eyes would adjust. When my eyes were finally adjusted, I found myself nose-to-nose with the upside-down face of a vampire bat. I ran out of the cave, screaming, and that was the end of my Dead Sea Scrolls expedition.

Creepy Tunnel Syndrome

Hezekiah's Tunnel is an ancient waterway connecting a valley spring outside of the walls of Jerusalem to the Pool of Siloam inside the walls.

Back in 1981, Hezekiah's Tunnel in Jerusalem was very primitive, and it was not the tourist site it is now. There was one security guard sitting on a folding chair and reading an Arabic language newspaper. At first, I thought I saw movement from the guard, but he just sat there on a folding chair next to the tunnel entrance. In 1981, things in that area seemed more tranquil than they do now.

> When there was a slight draft, our candles went out, leaving us in the pitch-black and knee-deep in dirty water.

Nowadays, I would have prepared by getting dressed like I was going fly-fishing in Wyoming, with those rubber pants that go from your toes to your armpits. But this is now, and that was then. Being foolhardy like every twenty-year-old, I was ready, wearing shorts and sandals. We also had no protection against critters.

The guard warned us that we needed flashlights, which Todd and I didn't have. Our solution was to go into the church in the nearby garden of Gethsemane and steal a couple of votive candles—the little ones with the paper around the top so the wax doesn't burn your hand.

As we ventured into the tunnel, the water was only ankle deep at first, but the tunnel was not level, and the water level fluctuated, reaching a high level at just above our knees. (Today, I wonder what creatures were in that water.)

When there was a slight draft, our candles went out, leaving us in the pitch-black and knee-deep in dirty water.

Naturally, we pressed forward in the dark, reasoning that we had come too far to turn back. What idiots. We accomplished this by putting one hand on each side of the tunnel and then just creeping forward, inch by inch.

Eventually, we saw a light at the end of the tunnel, went toward the light, and came out of the tunnel, soaking wet, in the middle of the Pool of Siloam. A group of French tourists was next to the pool with their guide, who was carrying her "Follow Me" umbrella. We just walked past them, as they were all rendered speechless.

Although it seemed like hours, we had been in the tunnel no more than fifteen minutes. One day I'll share this story as an illustration of the wisdom of being prepared. But for now, it is the best example I have to show the importance of having the teachings of the Bible at the ready, as they are the lamp unto our feet.

Almost as soon as I had declared my independence from Christ and the church, I underwent a severe test of my faith in Rome, Italy.

Italian Abduction.

In the early fall of 1981, after the trip to Israel, I spent the school year attending the Intercollegiate Center for Classical Studies in Rome, studying archaeology. The Centro, as we called it, was in the Trastevere (literally, "across the Tiber") section of Rome on the Vatican side but in a medieval section outside the ancient city.

One night a friend of mine from the Centro ventured out with me to watch *Superman* at the English-speaking movie theater in our neighborhood. The theater was located near a square famous for marijuana-smoking hippies, transients, and Eurail pass backpackers hanging out at all hours of the day and night. The movie ended at about 1:00 a.m., and my classmate and I began our walk back to the Centro.

While crossing the plaza, a Roman city police car (the little blue-and-white cars with Rome's city police inside, not the federal police) pulled up to the curb, and the police began shouting at us to get in the car. We had no idea why and didn't comply. The policemen got out and threw us in the back seat.

At first, we assumed we must be suspects for something we didn't do and that we were about to begin a scary adventure into the Roman legal system. We didn't think that we had done anything wrong, so we were not too scared or worried. Initially, we thought they must have us confused with somebody else, and they would take us to the station, perhaps to interview us, or book us, or something like that.

We soon understood, however, that our fate was to be far worse. Our Italian wasn't very good, but we understood enough to know that the two policemen couldn't decide where to turn at every intersection. One or the other would say, "Don't go right. No, go left. Go farther down and take a right after the third light." They clearly didn't know where they were going.

We realized we must not be going to the police station because the cops didn't know how to get to wherever they were taking us. Tremendous fear and dread—almost terror—immediately descended upon us. Something was going down that night—something terrible. Where were they taking us? Even they didn't seem to know.

We resolved that no matter what happened, we would not try to fight back, as they had guns. We didn't want to do anything that would cause them to use those guns.

> I thought of my mother, who would never know what had happened to me or know my whereabouts.

The car went south until it was in South Rome, many miles away. South Rome basically was the ghetto area of Rome. Then the car turned down an alley, and the policemen drove until they reached a clearing with railroad tracks. We were in an empty railroad yard in the middle of a ghetto in South Rome at two in the morning.

The policemen ordered us out of the car. We complied. They yelled at us in Italian—something like, "Why'd you do it?" When we responded, "Do what?" they struck us, backhanded, across the face. We fell on the ground, writhing in pain. They continued shouting as they kicked us, picked us up, and struck us again. I was repeatedly beaten, something I'd never experienced or imagined. I was sure this was the last night of my life.

I thought of my mother, who would never know what had happened to me or know my whereabouts.

No one knew where we were. No one would have known where to look. I would simply disappear. And the people responsible were the police.

Suddenly, three young people arrived. One appeared to be a woman, but the other two were men. They were dressed in long dark coats and spoke fluent English. (This was way before *The Matrix*. I know what you're thinking.)

The woman leaned over me on the ground and said, "Show him your ID."

I knew immediately what she meant. In my pocket was a photo ID card, showing I was registered with the Italian Department of Culture as an official "alien archaeologist." My ID had a very official-looking *La Republica d'Italia* stamp across my face. In truth, it was a fancy museum pass that allowed me to go for free to archaeology sites and to have nonpublic access. But when I pulled it out of my pocket and showed it to my attacker, he took one look at it, threw it on the ground, shouted to his colleague, jumped in the squad car, and sped away.

I'm not even sure if the policemen saw the young people in the black coats; it was confusing, and I was still on the ground, rolling around in agony at the time. (I suppose I could have hallucinated.)

Then I must have passed out because the only thing I remember after that moment was being in the back seat of a taxi, riding back to the nunnery where we lived.

My Thoughts and Interpretations

God answered my prayers—with power.

These young people didn't have wings. They didn't fly. They didn't hover over me in midair. But think about it—it was three o'clock in the morning in a railroad yard on the south side of Rome. Why would three Italian young people be walking around there?

Then they saw a Rodney King-style beating taking place, a police brutality event, and they intervened? What are the odds that they would have the courage to intervene in that set of circumstances?

And they spoke fluent English but also spoke to the policemen in fluent Italian. They knew that I had a pass—my "ID"—in my pocket. They knew I only had to show the cop the pass, and the cops would leave.

If you take any one of those circumstances, you might think it was a coincidence. But it's kind of like math—X times X times X times X times X is X to the fourth power. When you have that many strange, unexplainable circumstances—any one of which is unlikely to happen—and you combine them all in one event, the odds are astronomical. It's far easier to believe that they were my guardian angels than that it was a coincidence. God had his hand on me. He wasn't finished with me yet. I was twenty years old.

Back in the USA

After graduation, with seminary plans in the trash, I went to Washington, DC and was a legislative assistant to then-congressman Bill Lowery of San Diego for the next five years (1984-89). Part of that time overlapped with my going to law school at the University of Virginia.

During this time, I rarely attended church and was primarily focused on efforts to be successful, socially and professionally. My consuming sins were pride, ambition, and self-reliance—traits that, ironically, were viewed as virtues in my circles. I attended Fellowship Bible Church with my family when I visited Dallas, but I didn't have any Christian church or fellowship of any kind in DC.

I graduated from law school and was admitted to the bar in 1989. A year earlier, I'd met the woman who became my wife, Justine. Although Justine and I were first married in a civil ceremony 1988, we had a Christian wedding celebration ceremony in 1989 in Dallas. Justine is a native San Diegan and disliked the weather in Dallas, so we moved to San Diego in the fall of 1991.

In 1994, after my first son, Alexander was born, I determined to get back in fellowship with God. I had a period of repentance and began looking for a local church to attend. I had no idea how to find one, and in an era before Google searches, I went to a local Presbyterian church; we even took the membership class. In that class, we studied comic books that described the very basics of Christianity and the history of the Presbyterian church. We finished the class and were interviewed about our faith by one of the pastors, and then we publicly professed our faith in Christ in front of the whole congregation in a membership ceremony.

NOTES

Chapter 6

Parkinson's Diagnosis

Before I was afflicted, I went astray ... It is good for me that I was afflicted, that I might learn your statutes.

—Psalm 119:67, 71

It is for discipline that you have to endure. God is treating you as sons. For what son is there whom his father does not discipline? If you are left without discipline, in which all have participated, then you are illegitimate children and not sons. Besides this, we have had earthly fathers who disciplined us, and we respected them. Shall we not much more be subject to the Father of spirits and live? For they disciplined us for a short time as it seemed best to them, but he disciplines us for our good, that we may share his holiness. For the moment all discipline seems painful rather than pleasant, but later it yields the peaceful fruit of righteousness to those who have been trained by it. Therefore, lift your drooping hands and strengthen your weak knees, and make straight paths for your feet, so that what is lame may not be put out of joint but rather be healed.

—Hebrews 12:7–13

Right Index Finger.

In 1999, when I was thirty-eight years old, I went to the doctor at a walk-in urgent-care facility because of a little twitch on my right index finger. I thought maybe I was on the keyboard too much; maybe it was carpal tunnel syndrome. They sent me right up to neurology. Before I knew it, they were shooting electrical currents through me. I was prodded and poked and hammered and had wires all over my body.

What was going on? I was told three things could be causing my little finger flutter. Accordingly, the next step was to determine which of these doors I would walk through.

Door Number 1: Huntington's Disease

Huntington's disease is a deadly, genetic neurological disease. It is terminal and quick That didn't sound like a very good diagnosis to me. The doctor explained that it could be Huntington's Disease at least in part because of the presence of mental illness in my ancestry. She also advised that Huntington's Disease would likely be passed on to my children. Much to my discomfort, she wanted to test all three of my children! I refused that testing and reminded her that first, we needed to get my laboratory and DNA testing done. For the tests, I had to supply blood and urine to the Mayo Clinic, the world-famous medical research and treatment facility in Minnesota.

I complied with my requirement of supplying the doctor with blood and urine for their research. The tests would take no less than six weeks. I'd needed to wait more than six weeks to find out if I was going to die soon.

Then—can you believe it?—they lost my fluids. I had to make another donation, as it were. And I had to wait six more weeks! This was *brutal*.

In the end, I waited fifteen weeks for my final lab results which ruled out Huntington's Disease.

Door Number 2: Brain Cancer

About a week later, I was meeting with a client in my law office. I had been in an MRI tube for a brain scan the week before. My secretary runs into the meeting and whispers in my ear, "your doctor is on hold and she says it is urgent." I apologized to the client and cleared my office. I picked up the telephone and my neurologist quickly told me she'd found an anomaly in my MRI. "It might be brain cancer. We need to schedule you for an MRA— the subsequent scan— and a consultation with a neurosurgeon right away."

All I could think about it at that point was *How do I get a break from work to take an MRA?* I was thirty-eight years old and at the period of my life when work was all-consuming.

The MRA revealed no brain tumor, thankfully.

Door Number 3: Parkinson's Disease

Praise the Lord, but I got what was behind door number three. They call it young onset Parkinson's disease. This is the same thing that Michael J. Fox has.

As I said, I was thirty-eight; that was rough. If you're sixty-five or seventy, and you're diagnosed with Parkinson's, that's not good news. But when you lay a twenty-, thirty-, or forty-year decline estimate on someone who's already seventy, many of the issues with Parkinson's would occur after average life expectancy. When you're thirty-eight, you get to ride through all those times.

Parkinson's is incurable, progressive, and degenerative. It just gets worse. There are no Parkinson's survivors. It never lets go of you. It never goes away. I didn't have a lot of options for coping with the situation. I wasn't counting it as joy nearly two decades ago when I was diagnosed with young onset Parkinson's disease.

I was shocked. I had plans. I had goals. I had career objectives. I was doing well in my career. Everything I had worked so hard for was in the palm of my hand. My life was going great. I had all kinds of things lined up. My life was in order. Suddenly, I was told that in ten years, I'd be in a nursing home. I didn't have time for this! I had things to do.

I asked myself (not God), *Why is this happening to me? What did I do to deserve this?* My children were toddlers, and I thought, *Will I ever dance at my daughter's wedding?*

First came denial. *There must be a mistake. What else could cause these same symptoms?* Maybe there were more doors I could choose. Could it really be that Parkinson's was my best outcome?

Second, came anger. I complained, *"Why me? It is so unfair. I don't deserve this."* I was filled with anger. I paid my taxes. I hadn't hurt anyone. I wasn't out robbing banks or selling drugs. Why would God single me out for punishment?

Third, there came an emotional response reacting to my feeling that my getting Parkinson's was unjust. But this time I was thinking not that I would be spared, but that people more unworthy were not being diagnosed. I thought, *Why don't you punish that person? I don't like him very much, and he probably deserves it.* I named the names! You can understand what was going through my mind and how I would think that way, right? There are so many evil people in the world God could let get Parkinson's. *God, go turn your anger to those people.*

That's why the Prodigal Son story moved me so much—it was a story about a father still loving his son, even his disobedient son, and just wanting him to return to the family. The part about the father actually waiting at the gate for the return particularly moved my heart and moved my eyes to tears.

The real meaning to "perseverance of the saints" is not that you will not go astray but that God will welcome you back. Just come back. Come back.

Prodigal Returns

My mother is a saint. She's a real prayer-warrior. I often asked her to pray for me during those years because I thought the prayer of the righteous woman accomplishes much. "Would you ask God this for me?" I'd say. My friend Bruce Miller, whom I've known since elementary school, is a pastor in Dallas. He prayed for me every three months, every year I remained astray.

> It was a Sunday morning, and the auditorium was full, but when I heard Ray, it was like he was talking directly to me. It was like he and I were the only two people in the room.

Then in January 2000, I attended Maranatha Chapel, which is, ironically, five minutes from my house; I'd passed hundreds of times. Pastor Ray Bentley preached the Gospel message that day and said that the Father wants prodigals to come back—that we are not worthy, but He loves us anyway and wants us back.

God spoke to me that day.

I sat in the back. Pastor Ray Bentley was down front in the pulpit. It was a Sunday morning, and the auditorium was full, but when I heard Ray, it was like he was talking directly to me. It was like he and I were the only two people in the room.

I thought there was a cloud or fog covering all the other people's faces. I only saw Ray. And I rededicated my life to Jesus Christ there in Maranatha Chapel that day.

But I didn't get healed of Parkinson's.

My Thoughts and Views

I imagine our heavenly Father uses gradually ascending methods to get our attention, rising to whatever level is necessary.

During those years when I wasn't going to church, God reached out to me many times. I cannot say that God didn't call me back during those years, for I know he sent several messengers to me in the form of friends and family members. But I didn't listen. I knew people were praying for me.

What God does, I think, is sort of the same thing we do as parents. First, he starts off with a quiet inside voice. And he sends us subtle, gentle warnings. But if we ignore that, and we're children of God, he turns up the volume a little. And he keeps turning up the volume until he has our attention, just like we do with our own kids. He doesn't do this with everybody; he does only with his children.

I'm reminded that as a father, I have found it difficult to get my children's attention. My middle child has incredible powers of concentration that seem to leave him oblivious to my efforts. I begin calmly saying, "Spencer," and then I say his name again a little louder. Then a little louder; then—finally—I must shout *"Spencer!"*

I understand now, better than I ever could have before, that it is truly God who perseveres, even when we do not. His love is unfailing—not our love but his love. Look at the plain words of Jude 1:24: "Now to him who can keep you from stumbling and to present you blameless before the presence of his glory with great joy." From this verse, we must conclude that we, being sinners, are prone to stumble or, in any event, we could not possibly deliver ourselves as blameless before God. Thus, any notions we have about our eternal security in Christ are based on God's keeping us from falling. If it were up to us, we would all stumble, just as I did as a young man.

During my eighteen-year wandering in the wilderness, I was guilty not only of sins of commission—what I did—but also of sins of omission, or what I failed to do. As I look back, the sins of commission seem rather temporal, even momentary. The sins of omission—all those years out of fellowship and resisting God's will for my life—are what weigh most heavily on my conscience. All that lost time. So much I should have done (through God) but did not do!

NOTES

_____

_____

_____

_____

_____

_____

_____

_____

_____

_____

_____

_____

_____

_____

_____

Chapter 7

Why We Suffer

O Lord, rebuke me not in your anger,
nor discipline me in your wrath.
Be gracious to me, O Lord, for I am languishing;
heal me, O Lord, for my bones are troubled.
My soul also is greatly troubled.
But you, O Lord—how long
Turn, O Lord, deliver my life;
save me for the sake of your steadfast love.

—Psalm 6:1–4

Fifteen years ago, I was throwing the baseball with my son Spencer, then in his second year of T-ball. He was just learning to throw and catch. Although his dad was sure he saw a rocket arm, for all practical purposes, Spencer was still on the learning curve.

Although he was doing a good job of catching overall, one of the "pop flies" bounced off his glove and hit him smack in the face. He fell down crying. Ouch, that must have hurt.

I immediately ran to him and clutched him in my arms in an attempt to comfort him. He placed his arms around my neck and continued to cry. Then the following dialogue occurred:

Spencer: Daddy, why does God let things like that
happen? It's not fair.

Dad: I don't know, Spencer. I think sometimes God
    uses stuff that hurts us to teach us things.
Spencer: What is he trying to teach me?
Dad: Maybe he's just trying to teach you to keep
    your eye on the ball.
Spencer: Okay, then. I'll do that. Let's do it again.

There are some easy cases—a smoker gets lung cancer; that's likely to be a consequence of bad prior decisions—but there is still a mystery here too because reaping what you sow may be one of many interlocking reasons for your suffering. God can use the bad results of your bad decisions in such a way as to be for your benefit. In fact, that's exactly what he promises to do for us in Romans 8:28.

Eight Reasons We Suffer

It's not our job to ascertain the details of God's plan; our duty is to honor him and share his love and good news. Nonetheless, I have a list of the eight reasons for suffering that I have gleaned from the Bible and general human experience.

Each person suffering is on their own unique path, and no one can deny the experiences they have in suffering and recovery. But I have had a lot of opportunities to try to answer the question of why we suffer from the Bible's point of view. Without being overly dogmatic and except for suffering resulting directly from persecution on account of our faith in Jesus Christ, I believe we suffer because of one or all of the following:

1. It is the consequence of prior bad choices and behavior (law of sowing and reaping).

The examples here are the lung cancer patient who smoked cigarettes and the intravenous drug user who contracted AIDS or Hep C. This would also cover those who practiced any other

kind of reckless or negligent behavior. Essentially, we acknowledge that we will reap what we sow.

> Do not be deceived: God is not mocked, for what-
> ever one sows, that will he also reap. For the one
> who sows to his own flesh will from the flesh reap
> corruption, but the one who sows to the Spirit will
> from the Spirit reap eternal life. (Galatians 6:7–8)

There are at least two ways to look at the above verse. First,
it states the principle of the fruit of the poisoned root. That is, if
you sow one kind of thing, then you should expect to reap that
same thing if you repeat the same request as you did the first
time. Most of us get that. Second, if you sow, you must reap.
This principle is that you are responsible for the things you set
in motion. Second-hand smoke would be a good illustration.

2. It is Fatherly discipline for correction of believers.

The example here are the Christians who need to be unshackled
from repeated sin or sinful behavior, and God allows them to
suffer as a way of getting their attention.

> Consider him who endured from sinners such
> hostility against himself, so that you may not grow
> weary or fainthearted. In your struggle against sin,
> you have not yet resisted to the point of shedding
> your blood. And have you forgotten the exhorta-
> tion that addresses you as sons? My son, do not
> regard lightly the discipline of the Lord, nor be
> weary when reproved by him. For the Lord disci-
> plines the one he loves and chastises every son
> whom he receives.
>   It is for discipline that you have to endure.
> God is treating you as sons. For what son is there

whom his father does not discipline? If you are left without discipline, in which all have participated, then you are illegitimate children and not sons. Besides this, we have had earthly fathers who disciplined us, and we respected them. Shall we not much more be subject to the Father of spirits and live? For they disciplined us for a short time as it seemed best to them, but he disciplines us for our good, that we may share his holiness. For the moment all discipline seems painful rather than pleasant, but later it yields the peaceful fruit of righteousness to those who have been trained by it. (Hebrews 12:3–11)

This only applies to believers. Also available to believers is the option of God's kindness leading to repentance.[6]

3. God is getting your attention; he is drawing you closer.

The quickest way to get a man on his knees is by pulling the rug out from under his feet. Many of us have experienced this reason, as God uses trials to make us more humble, dependent on him, and prone to pray.

Being drawn closer means an intimate relationship is being restored. I observe that this reason may—and often does—overlap with other reasons. It is sort of a super-reason.

> God uses trials to make us more humble, dependent on him, and prone to pray.

As one example, note the immortal and much-loved words from Psalm 23:4–6, expressing what it means to be drawn closer by God:

---

[6] See also Romans 2:4.

Even though I walk through the valley of the
shadow of death,
I will fear no evil,
for you are with me;
your rod and your staff,
they comfort me.
You prepare a table before me
in the presence of my enemies;
you anoint my head with oil;
my cup overflows.
Surely goodness and mercy shall follow me
all the days of my life,
and I shall dwell in the house of the Lord.

4. God is equipping you for service.

The example of equipping is best observed by those who, having suffered from a trial, then find themselves able to minister to those who suffer from the same or similar afflictions.

Note where Paul describes one of the reasons we suffer—so we can comfort others:

> Blessed be the God and Father of our Lord Jesus Christ, the Father of mercies and God of all comfort, who comforts us in all our affliction, so that we may be able to comfort those who are in any affliction, with the comfort with which we ourselves are comforted by God. For as we share abundantly in Christ's sufferings, so through Christ we share abundantly in comfort too. If we are afflicted, it is for your comfort and salvation; and if we are comforted, it is for your comfort, which you experience when you patiently endure the same sufferings that we suffer. Our hope for you is unshaken, for we know that as you share in our

sufferings, you will also share in our comfort. (2 Corinthian 1:3–7)

5. God may have planned this to allow you to play a role in another person's life or for you to be a part of something much greater.

Members of a family often have group trials.

We may think we are the center of the galaxy, but often, we are on the periphery of something that grips the entire family. The importance of working together and suffering together must not be lost. Ecclesiastes 4:6–8 describes the need for facing hardships as a collective group. A cord of three strands is not quickly torn apart.

> We may think we are the center of the galaxy, but often, we are on the periphery of something that grips the entire family. The importance of working together and suffering together must not be lost.

6. Sin has effects in the world.

The example of this reason would be those who suffer because of plagues, earthquakes, tornadoes, hurricanes, etc., and those who are victims of murders, violence, and other wickedness.

> For I consider that the sufferings of this present time are not worth comparing with the glory that is to be revealed to us. For the creation waits with eager longing for the revealing of the sons of God. For the creation was subjected to futility, not willingly, but because of him who subjected it, in hope that the creation itself will be set free from its bondage to corruption and obtain the freedom of the glory of the children of God. For we know that the whole creation has been

groaning together in the pains of childbirth until now. (Romans 8:18–22)

7. For the glory of God, most likely by some gift or blessing you have received.

The example here is the man born blind.

> As he passed by, he saw a man blind from birth. And his disciples asked him, Rabbi, who sinned, this man or his parents, that he was born blind? Jesus answered, It was not that this man sinned, or his parents, but that the works of God might be displayed in him. (John 9:1–3)

8. We don't have a clue, so we must trust God.

The example here is every person who doesn't fit one of the reasons above.

We must never be judges who act like they can read other people's hearts and tell them the same things others have said to me:

> "God is disciplining you."
> "You are still sick because you have insufficient faith."
> "If you were in God's will, you wouldn't be suffering."

These statements are judgmental and wrong.

There are some easy cases of the consequence of bad prior decisions—again, that smoker who gets lung cancer—but there is still a mystery too because reaping what you sow may be one of many interlocking reasons for your suffering. God can use the bad results of your bad decisions in such a way as to be for your benefit. In fact, that's exactly what he promises to do for us in Romans 8:28 (more fully developed in the next chapter).

Finally, there are the pagan notions of why people suffer

and also philosophical approaches to this, some going back thousands of years; for example, karma. Many Christians believe and even teach karma, some unwittingly. Karma is the notion that ultimate balance and harmony will be achieved when good karma and bad karma coexist. One can believe and teach karma without ever using the word *karma*. It appears in these forms:

"He's got it coming to him."

"What goes around comes around."

"We are just following [restoring, protecting] the balance of nature."

"That misdeed sure came back to bite you."

We must remember that God is an intelligent being. He's not a force or a cosmic equation. He has a unique plan for all of us, and it doesn't just result from an algorithm designed to keep all events in balance. It results from God's love, and it addresses every prayer you have ever prayed.

NOTES

Chapter 8

He Works All Things for Our Good

And we know that for those who love God all
things work together for good, for those who are
called according to his purpose.

—Romans 8.28

Entire books have been written about Romans 8:28. This verse
about God's working everything for good may be the most frequently quoted scripture to those who are suffering and afflicted.

In some cases, the delivery of this message actually fans
the fires and is downright hurtful. But the world has many alternatives to Romans 8:28 that are not biblical and are quoted by
mindless by well-meaning Christians. For example, during an
ecumenical ceremony honoring those who died on 9/11, the
speaker misquoted God's Word by merely saying, "All things
work together for good."

Several important elements are missing from this misquote:
It is God who does the working. It's not a promise for everybody
but only for the called and those who love God. The good that
is worked together is God's good, which is according to his purpose. The good in this verse is what God considers to be "good",
not whatever "good" you desire or describe.

In some cases, we will never know what "good" results in
accordance with our being called according to his purpose. It
may main a mystery, at least in this life. Deuteronomy 29:29.:

says, "The secret things belong to the LORD our God, but the things that are revealed belong to us and to our children forever, that we may do all the words of this law."

Besides misquoting Romans 8:28, we also encounter many worldly alternatives for those seeking to tell someone that everything will turn out good. Below is a list of that worldly "wisdom" that is commonly offered for Romans 8:28 (but these are *not* what Romans 8:28 means):

1. *Every cloud has a silver lining.* The "good" in Romans 8:28 is not in the things themselves; it is in their divine purpose. It is in the plan God has for the things.
2. *Things just have a way of working themselves out for the best.* Romans 8:28 is not about benevolent fate. It's about a personal God who takes care of those who love him.
3. *If life hands you a lemon, make lemonade.* Romans 8:28 is not a command; it's a promise. The good that God purposes in the lives of the called is not dependent on human efforts.
4. *God helps those who help themselves.* God's promise in Romans 8:28 is unconditional and applies to those who are called and who love God, not those who are self-reliant.
5. *Trust God, but keep your gunpowder dry.* There are no exceptions or surprises for God. He works all things together for his good purposes.
6. *Be careful what you wish for; you just might get it.* We can be assured that the things in our lives truly work for good, even if they appear not to do so.

What Romans Promises and What it doesn't Promise:

- Romans 8:28 is not an excuse for human inaction.
- Romans 8:28 doesn't say all things are good.
- Romans 8:28 is not an algorithm (a problem-solving procedure, the set of rules a machine or a computer follows to achieve a particular goal. Romans 8:28 is not fate.

Things Actually Covered by Romans 8:28:

God works together all things which include:

- Your failures,
- Your mistakes,
- Your poor stewardship,
- Your derelictions of duties,
- Your lack of faith,
- Your inconsistency and unreliability,
- YOUR SINS!

Examples of God working together sins for a greater good:

- Jacob's being mistreated by Laban,
- Joseph being sold into slavery in Egypt,
- Joseph in prison with Pharaoh's cabinet,
- Moses flees to desert after a murder,
- Ruth, a Gentile wife of a Jew in violation of Mosaic Law, becomes a grandmother of David,
- David's adultery resulting in Bathsheba being an ancestor of Jesus.

Isn't this Fatalism? Isn't it Favoritism?

When imagining God's plan for our lives or when struggling with God's sovereignty being used selectively to ensure that only those who love God and are called according to his purpose will benefit—especially before loading the debate and argument guns—it is advisable to take a moment to worship God and remind ourselves of how much above our understanding God truly is.

No illustration I could ever conceive would do justice to the vastness of the universe, let alone God, its Creator. Nevertheless, I have a story from my experiences that might be helpful.

The Dog Box

In the late 1980s, when Justine and I were newly married, we lived on the fourteenth floor of a condo high-rise on McKinney Avenue near downtown Dallas. I worked as an associate at Baker & Botts, and Justine worked as a paralegal at Thompson & Knight. We had two small Yorkshire terriers: one I adopted upon marrying Justine called Corky and one I named Calvin.

Because Justine and I were both at work all day, we kept Corky and Calvin in the kitchen with the doors closed, as this was the only room in the condo that wasn't carpeted. The little guys had tiny bladders and had to hold themselves from about eight in the morning until seven in the evening. By the time we got home, they were ready to burst, but we couldn't just open the door and let them out to do their business—we were on the fourteenth floor of a posh condo tower.

So what did we do?

We had a dog carrier and ordered the dogs to "Get in the box! Get in the box!"

The dogs were very excited to see us, and we were happy to see them, but with their little bladders stretched to their limits, I wasn't about to pick them up or let them jump on my nice work clothes. Rather than greeting them with open arms, I ordered them into the dog carrier.

At first, the dogs were reluctant to get in the box, but after repeating my command, they eventually learned they had no choice but to obey. Once in the box, of course, we had to ride the elevator down to the basement, walk through the garage, climb steps, and finally emerge in the designated dog area out-side the building. There, I would release them from their cage, and they would do their business at last. I petted them, and we played. The time for celebration eventually came but only after a strange journey down and up while confined in a box.

Why have I told this story? Well, I was completely aware of the circumstances; I knew they had full bladders. I knew they were happy to see me and couldn't control themselves in such circumstances. I knew the building management didn't want dog pee on the hallway carpet. I knew my neighbors didn't want their shoe polish blemished. I knew the only way to keep them from all that was to put them in the box and thereby assure their continued happy residence in the building.

But what did the dogs understand? They knew their bladders were full and that their master, after a long absence, only wanted them caged. Nothing more. Could these dogs have possibly comprehended what my dry-cleaning bill would be if they soiled my suit? Could they have ever read the lease and known one of the grounds for eviction was not controlling the behavior of animals? Could they have understood where I was taking them as they rode down that elevator? Could they have known how long the journey in the box would last? When they got in the box, did they know it would take minutes? Did they even know where I was taking them?

> I now thank God for my Parkinson's disease, for God—praise his name—used it to get my attention. He used it to turn me around.

No, they could have understood none of this. They just had to learn to trust me, obey me, and believe that I was caring for them. After a few such experiences, as soon as I arrived home, they would run right into the box—the only place they wanted to be right then.

Consider this: there is a huge gap in understanding between my dogs and me in the meaning and purpose of my ordering them into the box, so imagine how much greater is the gap in the understanding of life's events, trials, and tribulations between us and our sovereign, omniscient God of the universe.

Next time you find yourself in the box, trust and obey God. He is caring for you. After a while, your trust will become strong enough that you may properly consider that box to be the best place for you at that particular moment in time.

I now thank God for my Parkinson's disease, for God—praise his name—used it to get my attention. He used it to turn me around. He does work all things together for good for those who love him and who are called according to his purpose.

NOTES

Chapter 9

Coping with Parkinson's Disease

Of such a one will I glory: yet of myself I will not glory but in mine infirmities. For though I would desire to glory, I shall not be a fool; for I will say the truth: but now I forbear, lest any man should think of me above that which he seeth me to be, or that he heareth of me. And lest I should be exalted above measure through the abundance of the revelations, there was given to me a thorn in the flesh, the messenger of Satan to buffet me, lest I should be exalted above measure. For this thing, I besought the Lord thrice, that it might depart from me. And he said unto me, my grace is sufficient for thee: for my strength is made perfect in weakness. Most gladly, therefore, will I rather glory in my infirmities, that the power of Christ may rest upon me. Therefore, I take pleasure in infirmities, in reproaches, in necessities, in persecutions, in distresses for Christ's sake: for when I am weak, then am I strong.

—2 Corinthians 12:5–10

Strengthen ye the weak hands and confirm the feeble knees. Say to them that are of a fearful heart, be strong, fear not: behold, your God will

come with vengeance, even God with a recom-
pense; he will come and save you. Then the eyes
of the blind shall be opened, and the ears of the
deaf shall be unstopped. Then shall the lame man
leap as a hart, and the tongue of the dumb sing:
for in the wilderness shall waters break out, and
streams in the desert.

—Isaiah 35:3–6

Developing Parkinson's disease at age thirty-eight caused my
entire life to change. At the time of my return to the fold, the
conviction of my heart was to restore my witness, get back in
fellowship, restore Christ as my personal Lord (not just Savior),
and to undertake to save my children, whom I felt hadn't yet
heard the Gospel.

I still don't know with certainty why I have Parkinson's. But
I do know this: the Lord used my Parkinson's. God took me off
my high horse, as I'd say in Texas. He used it to bring me back.

I continue to suffer every day, but God is using Parkinson's to
restore in me a form of holiness and faith that honors his name.
I pray repeatedly to be healed, but so far, Christ has said that his
grace alone is sufficient for me and that through my infirmity, I
will be made strong.

Praise be to God for his goodness and love and grace for
seeing me in the pigpen, inviting me back to his house, and
having a welcome banquet for me. Truly, he loves me as only a
father could.

Coping with Parkinson's

A few years ago, I received a call from a long-time client, not
about legal advice but something more important—although I
didn't know that at the time. We made arrangements to have
lunch, and he picked me up in his Ferrari; he was a very successful businessman and venture capitalist. I was impressed.

When we arrived at the restaurant in the posh neighborhood

of Rancho Santa Fe in San Diego, he greeted the proprietor by his first name. The proprietor then mentioned that all the arrangements had been made, and they were ready to serve us on the terrace. I was again very impressed.

We were shown to our seats immediately, and then I realized that my client had reserved the entire terrace and had the door to the main dining area closed. Mind you, I'd had a lot of clients show off by ordering custom preparations that weren't on the menu, but this seemed more like a scene in a Robert Ludlum novel where the protagonist first encounters the international conspiracy's cabal or star chamber—but that would be my imagination getting the better of me. My client just wanted complete privacy.

Then, sometime between the soup and the pasta courses, I came right to the point and asked him plainly, "What would you like to discuss?"

He tasted the pasta and drank some wine, and then he said, "It is about coping strategies or, more specifically, *your* coping strategies." He said he was aware of my faith in Jesus Christ and my reliance on the Bible. "I've known you've had Parkinson's disease for several years, but I haven't thought much about it until now."

Still not comprehending what this was about, I asked, "Why do you want to know?"

The response I got was, "I have leukemia, a variant that is not treatable, and the doctors say I have just a few more years to live."

The first thing that went through my mind was how sorry for him I was. His children were in preschool. The second thing was how deceptive wealth can be. I'd admired his car and his overall wealth and had thought; *Some guys just have all the luck.* I was wrong, and it made me wonder how many other people I'd misjudged because of superficialities.

Some guys just have all the luck. I was wrong, and it made me wonder how many other people I'd misjudged because of superficialities.

The third thing that went through my mind was how inexcusably unprepared I was to answer this man who sought to learn the reason for my joy and hope. What were my coping strategies? I wasn't sure, but I mentioned something about taking one day at a time.

Later, I felt I'd failed this test. Was that really all I had to offer this man with terminal cancer?

My PD

I resolved then to better understand how I viewed my illness and how God had enabled me to be truly joyful while afflicted by an incurable, degenerative, disabling, and potentially even fatal disease, officially called young onset Parkinson's disease.

I took a step back and realized everyone has the same questions. Everyone needs a coping strategy. Everyone wonders "why me?" and most of us wonder "why not me?" Each and every disabled person must spend lots of time going over a thousand what-ifs. The one with the brain disease certainly fears for her future. And nearly everyone with faith in God finds that faith put to the test; often, the faith is too weak to endure.

> Yet there are people who find joy in the middle of a trial or affliction. We have to ask, "Why does this person feel happy while in pain?"

Yet there are people who find joy in the middle of a trial or affliction. We have to ask, "Why does this person feel happy while in pain?"

Every person who develops Parkinson's disease (PD) gets his or her own unique version of it. After nineteen years of fighting it, some of my symptoms include tremors, stiffness, shuffling of feet, feeling very cold, double vision, hallucinations, loss of smell and taste, drooling, dry mouth, slurred speech and soft talking loss of balance, falling, a decline in memory and cognitive skills, a decline in hand and feet dexterity, and chronic pain.

OVERCOMING THE TRIALS OF A LIFETIME

It doesn't sound like much, but compared to what was predicted, it's a clear victory. Medical science promises great advances in the treatment and possible cure of Parkinson's disease in my lifetime. As of this writing, however, there is no cure or even any medicine arresting its progression. All I do is attempt to control symptoms by ingesting greater and greater portions of chemicals, each with their side effects.

Some of What PD Has Taught Me

As I observe my mind gradually becoming disconnected from my body, while I live within the body and observe the phenomenon, I'm reminded that our bodies are not us; they are but earthen vessels. As I watch my arm shake without responding to any command of my consciousness, I rest assured that *truly* we have eternal souls, and we are not mere flesh and blood.

We ourselves are not the flesh; the flesh merely contains us. I can see this visibly in my own self. I long for the new body like Christ's that I've been promised.

Double Whammies

One of the mistakes some people make when they have an incurable, degenerative, and chronic disease like Parkinson's is to assume it's the only trial they will have to endure. It is sort of like the expression, "Lighting never strikes twice in the same place." But it does. Sometimes people even add Alzheimer's for a real double whammy. That is not my case, as of yet, but I can only pray and wait on the Lord.

In the meantime, I have had to endure breathtaking pain twice.

About seven years ago, I came down with shingles. If you ever had chicken pox, then you are a candidate for developing shingles. Get the shot to prevent it because shingles may be the most painful experience you will ever have.

For me, it meant I had scab-like sores and boils all across my back, most of which I could not reach. The pain comes from all the nerves misfiring under the surface of the skin or sores, giving you the realistic feeling of your flesh having been set ablaze. My pain was so acute that I literally screamed. This goes on for weeks—for me, it was six weeks—and there is almost nothing you can do about it.

The second double whammy I suffered was a herniated disk/lumbar stenosis and sciatica. In my case, the first symptoms appeared while I was on a cruise with my oldest son, who was twenty-three at the time. Essentially, two of my vertebrae were rubbing against each other and pinching my sciatic nerves, sending excruciating pain down my legs from hip to heel. During those months, I was prescribed several acute pain-reliever medicines, to which I became addicted.

After several epidural shots that were all fruitless, I was scheduled for surgery to fuse the two vertebrae together, away from the nerve. Thankfully, the surgery appears to have been mostly successful. I also went cold turkey on the painkillers and shook off the addiction.

Don't Go It Alone

When I was growing up in Texas, my parents thought the city kid needed some exposure to country living (or maybe they just wanted me out of the house), so most summers as a child, I attended a ranch camp. Ranch camp mostly consisted of riding horses who followed trails they already knew, interrupted by swimming in the swimming pool or attending rodeos.

Typically, ranch camp sessions ended with a genuine Texas barbecue, and the highlight of the day was the all-camp tug-of-war. A huge, thick rope stretched across a filthy cow pond (unconfirmed rumors were that the cow pond contained "boa constrictors"). Being on the losing team obviously was a very unpleasant experience. One summer, one of the boys found a leech attached to him in about the worst place a boy could imagine!

Everybody knows the key to a tug-of-war victory is *before* the tug-of-war even begins; it's in the selection of the teams. Simply put, if one team had stronger (or fatter) members or even more members—the teams almost always were unbalanced—that team would win … and the losers would end up in the cow pond.

Sometimes in the Christian life, we imagine a spiritual or moral tug-of-war taking place, usually between our flesh and our new nature. Most of us believe that upon regeneration, our wills will no longer be enslaved, and—as the Latin theologians used to say—we will have the ability to sin and the ability not to sin. Of course, we often assume these abilities are equally matched. We can't help remembering the television shows and cartoons we saw as children showing a little devil and a little angel inside our souls, competing equally for our decisions.

But I don't think the spiritual tug-of-war involves two equally matched opponents; I think it's like the one at Ranch Camp. It isn't an equal decision between two equally matched opponents. The key is who's on the righteous team and who's on the sinful team.

On one side are the habits of the flesh, the temptations of the world, the things that make us proud or boastful, lusts of the eyes, materialistic temptations, and desires, idols, and so forth. On the other side is prayer, reading the Bible, fellowship with other Christians, ministering to others, and so on.

I don't want to leave the impression it's about works, but at the human level, if we load up the fleshly team, for example, with exposure to sin, worldly surroundings, and temptations of the eyes, we are picking a strong team for that side of the tug-of-war. If we abide in Christ, pray regularly and fervently, meditate on his Word, and exhale by ministering and witnessing to others, we strengthen the righteous team.

Likewise, if we expunge our daily schedule from worldly temptations, we weaken the team of the flesh. If we neglect prayer, Bible study, church, or sharing, we weaken the team of the spirit. If we have a strong flesh team and a weak spirit team, would it be any surprise to end up in the cow pond?

I feel that in my own life when I have strayed from Christ, I've found myself mired in sin, and I usually can look back and say, "Hey, you bonehead, no wonder you stumbled. Look at your teams! You had big, strong flesh-team members, and you weren't praying, you weren't in the Word, and you weren't in fellowship with God or other Christians. You should have seen it coming."

God has promised that he will not place us in trial or temptation that we cannot bear, but perhaps that means that all the spirit-team members are right there, looking at us, bouncing up and down saying, "Pick me. Pick me." If we fail to pick them and succumb to the temptation, God has kept his word. He gave us the strength to resist or pass through the trial; we just picked the wrong team.

Each day is a new tug-of-war, and we get to pick our teams. Pick your players carefully. The stronger team wins.

Urgency

My PD makes me feel like I'm living with a ticking clock, a feeling few my age have in the same way I do. I have an inescapable feeling that time is running out, that the hourglass will soon be empty. A sense of urgency overwhelms me.

Every day is the last day for some of us. Others are suffering, as I was, and are ripe to hear his Word, not one day but today. We must share his good news with a sense of urgency.

I trust God and his Word. What follows now in this book are the results of my quest for answers to my many questions. I hope they will also answer some of yours.

NOTES

Chapter 10

Pray to Be Healed

Heal me, O Lord, and I shall be healed; save me, and I shall be saved, for you are my praise.
—Jeremiah 17:14

When thinking about the power of prayer my memory always goes to one Sunday morning, about a decade ago or more with a scene from my two boys' younger days. By my best estimate, my oldest, Alex was about 10 and Spencer was about 8 years old.

I was late driving us to church, and to compound the problem, I was teaching that morning and I just couldn't be late. I drove as aggressively as I could, but I had to stop what seemed to be every single red light.

I began praying out loud something like

Dear Heavenly Father, I am your servant and I thank you for the many blessings you have granted. But forgive me, Lord God, if I ask for one more blessing? Can you please give me some green lights? Not all the time, just when I'm trying to get to church and especially when I am teaching. Please, Lord, give me green lights.

Unexpectedly Spencer ventured a theological problem-solving method. Spencer said, Dad just ask for red lights and God will give you green lights. That's how it works." Could reverse psychology work on God? Not a chance.

Then Alex took the cake when in soft deadpan he said, "Why don't you just adjust your alarm clock, so you get up earlier." Always the practical one.

By the way, empirical data failed to resolve it, because the rest of the way to church, I got a mix of reds, greens, and yellows.

Withered Leg

When one of my sons was younger, he was in Awana, a great children's discipleship program. I helped him with his weekly exercises, and one week his assignment was to pray for someone in his house, a grandparent, and a parent. So he picked our dog, my stepfather, and me.

Here's what he prayed:

"Dear God, I hope our dog will get his eyes better, so he can see again and not be blind. God, I hope Grandpa's polio leg will get better and be normal again. [His grandpa had polio in the 1940s.] Dear God, I hope Daddy's left ear will work again, and he won't be deaf in it anymore." I had mumps at age seven and lost the hearing in my left ear.

I listened to my son's prayer, and when he prayed, it was clear his God could do anything—absolutely anything; not even the sky was the limit. Beyond imagination is what his God could do, and so I thought, *Wait a minute—I need to talk to him. He hasn't been around the block like I have. He isn't praying for stuff that might happen. I don't want him to be disappointed.*

> Although his God could do anything, my God was in a box that I constructed, based on what I thought God could do.

Although his God could do anything, my God was in a box that I constructed, based on what I thought God could do. I thought God could do whatever was inside the box, but whatever was outside the box was beyond God's reach.

Prayer Changes Things

My mom and my friend Bruce kept on praying, and their faith was tested, but eventually, their prayers were answered. My story and my rededication to Christ in January 2000 was a story of prayer, a story of people who didn't give up on friends or loved ones who fell away from the faith for years. These prayers were answered, for God used my Parkinson's diagnosis to soften my hard heart and make it ready again to hear the Word.

Prayer Is Not a Moot Point

The smart but unwise Bible student asks the question, "If God already has a plan, what difference do our prayers make? Why should we bother?"

It is certain that God hears and answers our prayers, even in eternity past.

Before the foundation of the world, God heard your prayers. There never was a time when he did not hear your prayers. There never was a time when he didn't have a plan for your life. His plan for you is his answer to all your prayers; your prayers are answered in his plan. In the plan he wrote, he was fully aware of your prayers. And that plan is revealed to you in prayer and in your life as it unfolds.

Let's move past this question of plans versus prayers and get on our knees and start praying.

Here's my view on how we should go about praying for healing by God, in his mercy.

Be Devoted to Prayer

Take note of Colossians 4:2, which says, "Continue steadfastly in prayer, being watchful in it with thanksgiving." *Continue steadfastly* is often translated as "be devoted," meaning ardent, dedicated, loyal, and zealous. Being devoted means it's a priority;

you put some effort and preparation into it, and maybe you even put some blood, sweat, and tears into it.

Sometimes the Greek word is translated as "persevere in prayer," and that's a common description of prayer in the New Testament. For example, in Acts 1:14, the early church was all of one mind, and the believers were "continually devoting themselves to prayer."[7] Likewise, Paul uses Romans 12:12 to command us to "be devoted to prayer," and uses Ephesians 6:18 to tell us to "Pray at all times in the Spirit ... with all perseverance."

To me, being devoted means being a zealous advocate who wants to make the strongest case for prayer that I can. Make your best argument and plead with him. Quote scripture back to God. That's biblical. Show him you care about his answer, and then later, when you have waited, let him know you still care.

Be Alert in Prayer

Keeping "alert" in prayer means, first and foremost, that you stay awake. Besides that, work against distractions and hindrances. Do whatever you have to do to stay on the task. It also means that you should listen to God's feedback, look for God's answer, and—again, very important—stay awake.

> Keeping "alert" in prayer means, first and foremost, that you stay awake. Besides that, work against distractions and hindrances.

Be Thankful in Prayer

Praying "with thanksgiving" means you thank God now, not later. At the moment when you are praying, you should be thankful to him for (1) listening to your prayer, (2) answering according to his will, even though you don't yet know what that answer is, and (3) giving you the privilege of including your requests in his divine plan.

---

[7] See also Acts 2:42; 6:4.

Remember: God is not a Coke machine. You don't just press the button and get what you want. But also remember:

> Likewise, the Spirit helps us in our weakness. For we do not know what to pray for as we ought, but the Spirit himself intercedes for us with groanings too deep for words. And he who searches hearts knows what is the mind of the Spirit because the Spirit intercedes for the saints according to the will of God. (Romans 8: 26–27)

This means that if you're barely able to pray, or you don't know how to pray with confidence or boldly approach the throne, or you lack the assurance needed to "name it and claim it," and/or all of those things you think you want to and should do, then take heart—the Holy Spirit, who indwells every believer, will step up and pray for you.

Pray with a Godly Attitude

First, *get right with God*. Don't expect God's power to rescue you from the intentional sin you're harboring and not give up.[8]

Second, *remember to pray, "Not my will but your will be done."*

Third, *be patient and wait for the Lord*. There is a strong connection throughout the Bible between making requests of God and waiting patiently for God to answer. For example, Psalm 27:14 says, "Wait for the Lord; Be strong and let your heart take courage; Wait for the Lord." This link between praying and waiting is especially evident in the psalms.[9]

> But for you, O Lord, do I wait;
> it is you, O Lord my God, who will answer.
> (Psalm 38:15)

---

[8] See Isaiah 40:29, Psalm 10:17.
[9] See also Psalm 33:20; 40:1; 119:166.

I wait for the Lord, my soul waits,
and in his word, I hope; my soul waits for the Lord
more than watchmen for the morning.
(Psalm 130:5)

Consequently, we can't expect that every time we ask God for something, he will do it instantaneously or even quickly.

God has his timing, which often is not our timing. And even if we knew in advance how long it would take, we would not be patient. We need to learn to wait patiently for the healing of our bodies.

> And not only the creation, but we ourselves, who have the first fruits of the Spirit, groan inwardly as we wait eagerly for adoption as sons, the redemption of our bodies. For in this hope we were saved. Now hope that is seen is not hope. For who hopes for what he sees? But if we hope for what we do not see, we wait for it with patience. (Romans 8:23–25)

Isaiah 40:31 tells us, "But with wings like eagles; they shall run and not be weary; they shall walk and not faint." But you know what? We always skip the waiting part. It says these miracles are for those who wait; those who wait for the Lord.

> We can't expect that every time we ask God for something, he's will do it instantaneously or even quickly.

- Sometimes God does not answer instantaneously.
- Sometimes God answers later.
- Sometimes his answer is gradually revealed to you.

Fourth, *let God know how much you care by making the best case for what you are asking for.* We won't conform to the mind of Christ if we don't include an explanation of why we are asking God for something. Follow these steps:

- Show him you care.
- Be clear on what you care about.
- Tell him why you care
- Later, tell him you still care.

See the appendix for a sample prayer for another person's healing.

NOTES

Chapter 11

When It Seems Unfair

This is my comfort in my affliction,
that your promise gives me life.

—Psalm 119:50

And when Jesus saw their faith, he said to the
paralytic, Son, your sins are forgiven.

—Mark 2:5

Jesus Could Have Healed Me

One Easter weekend, I enjoyed watching some classic movies with my children. One of them was *The Robe*, starring Richard Burton as the unsaved Roman tribune Marcellus Aelius Gallio, who crucified Christ. Another was *Ben-Hur*. I highly recommend both movies for the whole family. They don't make movies like they used to—that's for sure—but one scene in *The Robe* really struck me as amazingly profound.

If you've ever been ill or faced with adversity or a trial, and your prayers for healing seem not to have been answered—as I have felt from time to time, I'll readily admit—then consider the following scene from *The Robe*:

The scene takes place shortly before Marcellus's conversion to Christianity. He is speaking to a Christian girl in Cana named Miriam. Miriam was paralyzed when she met Jesus, but Jesus did not heal her paralysis. Nevertheless, Marcellus saw her singing of her joy of faith to an assembly of Christians and was puzzled. (I pick up the dialogue after the conversation already started):

> Miriam: Jesus is alive, more surely than we are. He taught us to love God with all our hearts and one another as ourselves.
>
> Marcellus: Worlds are built on force, not charity. Power is all that counts.
>
> Miriam: Perhaps we have something better than power. We have hope.
>
> Marcellus (*with great emphasis*): That you of all people should say that! You can see [pointing to her crippled legs] that he [Jesus] left you just as he found you!
>
> Miriam: I used to wonder about that myself until faith taught me the answer. He could have healed my body, and then it would have been natural for me to laugh and sing. And then I came to understand that he had done some-thing even better for me. He had chosen me for his work. He left me as I am so that all oth-ers like me might know that their misfortune needn't deprive them of happiness within his kingdom.
>
> Marcellus: It is beyond reason that anyone should think as you do!
>
> Miriam: Not if you had only known him, looked into his eyes, or heard him speak.

This short scene in the movie made an impression on me. From our human point of view, as mentioned in *The Robe*, it is "beyond reason" that anyone would be joyous about being par-alyzed, yet with faith in God and who he is, this joy makes all the sense in the world.

This scene is a good example of what dealing with adversity

is about, and that is understanding that God is sovereign, and he has his purpose in the events in our lives, including diseases, adversities, and trials. We should rejoice in these events and tribulations, knowing that God's purposes are loving and just.

Time to Time

"Why didn't he answer the way I asked him—right away?"

"What if God doesn't heal me—ever?"

God's timing is not our timing. Many times, we are so convinced of the accuracy of our timetable that we actually conclude that God has not answered our prayers—because he didn't do so on our schedule.

In this frame of mind, late healing appears to be no healing. We think gradual healing is no healing. Any kind of delay in accordance with God's timetable is seen as a rejection of our request.

I think this often happens because we are so focused on our lives and the world that we fail to see—much less understand—all the ways God is telling us to adjust our timing to his timing.

Peter shares the same eternal, even heavenly, perspective:

> Blessed be the God and Father of our Lord Jesus Christ! According to his great mercy, he has caused us to be born again to a living hope through the resurrection of Jesus Christ from the dead, to an inheritance that is imperishable, undefiled, and unfading, kept in heaven for you, who by God's power are being guarded through faith for a salvation ready to be revealed in the last time. In this you rejoice, though now for a little while, if necessary, you have been grieved by various trials, so that the tested genuineness of your faith— more precious than gold that perishes though it is tested by fire—may be found to result in praise and glory and honor at the revelation of Jesus Christ.

> Though you have not seen him, you love him.
> Though you do not now see him, you believe in
> him and rejoice with joy that is inexpressible and
> filled with glory, obtaining the outcome of your
> faith, the salvation of your souls. (1 Peter 1:3—9)

Again, note the words of the psalmist: "For his anger is but for a moment, and his favor is for a lifetime. Weeping may tarry for the night, but joy comes with the morning" (Psalm 30:5).

Here are my five healing principles when you're trying to resolve the question of why you are suffering:

Healing Principle No. 1: God's Healing of a Soul Is a Greater Miracle than Healing a Body.

I can only speculate what my life would have been like if something had been different, but I'm going to do it anyway. If God had healed me instantly the first time that I asked him to heal me from Parkinson's, I'd be a different person today than I am now. I would have had different experiences, different challenges, a different outlook, a different attitude. I would not have learned to trust God, in the same way, I do now.

> Healing my soul was more important and a greater miracle than the healing of my body.

Sometimes, healing my soul was more important and a greater miracle than the healing of my body.

And through the weakness of my body, my soul became stronger. It's God's power in me; don't misunderstand.

Read the powerful words from Ephesians 3:14—21.[10]

> For this reason I bow my knees before the Father,
> from whom every family in heaven and on earth
> is named, that according to the riches of his glory

------
[10] See also Acts 3:1—8; 2 Timothy 4:16—17.

he may grant you to be strengthened with power through his Spirit in your inner being that Christ may dwell in your hearts through faith—that you, being rooted and grounded in love, may have strength to comprehend with all the saints what is the breadth and length and height and depth, and to know the love of Christ that surpasses knowledge, that you may be filled with all the fullness of God. Now to him who is able to do far more abundantly than all that we ask or think, according to the power at work within us, to him be glory in the church and in Christ Jesus throughout all generations, forever and ever. Amen.

God's plan for you is perfect! Try as you might, you can't make one better.

Healing Principle No. 2: When God Doesn't Immediately Heal, He Gives You the Strength to Make It Through.

Colossians 1:11 states, "May you be strengthened with all power, according to his glorious might, for all endurance and patience with joy." Paul asked God to give us endurance and patience. These virtues only come with waiting. There's an important lesson here. Remember we have a tendency, culturally, to think everything must be instant; we want "drive-through" grace. Give our order at the first window, pay at the next window, and get our food at the third window, all while the clock measures the progress. God doesn't provide drive-through grace.

We may think that if we pray for somebody that God must answer instantly. If we pray on Tuesday for someone with cancer, then we expect there'll be no cancer on Wednesday. This is an attitude we have brought from our childhoods—an expectation of instant gratification.

Healing Principle No. 3: God Doesn't Usually Zap Us with Healing Power; More Often He Strengthens Our Muscles.

Sometimes God does not immediately heal, but he'll use the experience to make you stronger. According to the Old Testament prophet Isaiah:

> He gives power to the faint, and to him who has no might he increases strength. Even youths shall faint and be weary, and young men shall fall exhausted, but they who wait for the Lord shall renew their strength; they shall mount up with wings like eagles; they shall run and not be weary; they shall walk and not faint. (Isaiah 40:29–31)

And again, in Isaiah 41:10: "Fear not, for I am with you; be not dismayed, for I am your God; I will strengthen you, I will help you, I will uphold you with my righteous right hand."

God doesn't want to make your life easier. He wants to make you stronger. Colossians 1:29 states, "For this I toil, struggling with all his energy that he powerfully works within me."

We're struggling; we're toiling, laboring, or agonizing, and he gives us the power to do that, but our muscles are getting stronger. Why is that good? Because we can hold the other person up.

As a result, sometimes people are healed, and other times people go to physical therapy. The final result is that all believers will be healed, but each of us has our own unique path to get there.

Healing Principle Number 4: When God Doesn't Immediately Heal, It May Be to Work a Greater Miracle.

When God doesn't immediately heal, it may be to work a greater miracle than healing you. Now remember when I say heal, I'm talking about physical infirmities, but I am also talking about broken relationships and financial struggles. All the trials you experience are covered by this. And if he doesn't immediately fix it, maybe it is to work a greater miracle.

When you go through a trial, you're a witness for Christ. In fact, you're a witness whether you like it or not because people are watching you. You're going through a trial. This is the best opportunity to be a witness that you can have. Because you can thank God for his mercy and his grace in bringing you through that trial.

> My sister-in-law is a breast cancer survivor. I saw her when she was going through chemo when she had no hair. She was in the best of spirits. I said, "How's the treatment?" She said, "It's so wonderful. I have so many witnessing opportunities."
>
> She went through chemo and was praising the Lord for witnessing opportunities. While I was there, she got a letter from the American Cancer Society, asking her to go on the road to give pep talks to women with breast cancer. She cried when she got the letter. She said, "What a mission God has given me."

You can praise the Lord as Job did. Don't ever curse the Lord but praise the Lord. Job's refusal to curse God when his family had been killed was an awesome witness. You can be a witness, too. And it's a powerful witness especially to people who are going through the same thing as you are.

You could think of a trial as an opportunity, a sickness as a challenge, and a financial struggle as a stewardship.

Healing Principle No. 5: When God Doesn't Immediately Heal, He May Be Healing You Gradually

This one is my favorite. I was reading sermons on power, but I didn't find a lot of preachers talking about gradual healing. I think

God does that a lot. I think a lot of times we want the whole thing fixed immediately—over and done.

God has a plan for you.

If you're in physical therapy to help you to walk again, and you succeed, is that any less of a miracle?

Maybe God wants you to go through six months or a year of physical therapy to strengthen your soul and faith and prayer muscles, as well as your physical muscles. Maybe you need a period of dependence and closeness with Christ. God can heal you gradually. His grace is sufficient.

The truth is that every believer will be healed. All those who put their trust in Christ and his work on the cross will be healed at the resurrection of all believers. The difference is that we all have our unique pathways to get to that same destination.

Don't misunderstand—I am not saying all religions are equal or lead to the same result. Rather, I am saying that God has a customized individual life plan for each of us. For some that include miraculous healings, and for others, it involves long and painful recoveries.

> If you're in physical therapy to help you to walk again, and you succeed, is that any less of a miracle?

God loves all of us, and he has determined what is best for us because he knows us better than we know ourselves. And as we will see, his plans for us are better than we could have asked or imagined.

Examples of Claiming the Promises

Heavenly Father,

I believe your promise that when we ask for a thorn in the flesh to be removed, and it is not removed, that this is so, in our own weakness, we should be made strong by relying only on you and to the glory of your name.

Heavenly Father, you promised us that if we ask anything in the name of Jesus that is according to your will that you will grant our requests and hold no good thing back from us. Believing that promise, I ask all these things in the name of Jesus Christ, your Son and my Lord.

NOTES

Chapter 12

Experience God's Power

Remember not the sins of my youth
or my transgressions;
according to your steadfast love remember me,
for the sake of your goodness, O Lord!

—Psalm 35:7

Praise His Power.

Listen to Psalm 21:13: "Be exalted, O Lord, in your strength! We will sing and praise your power."[11] God is all-powerful, and God wants to be praised for his power. We worship him for his mercy; we worship him for his justice; we worship him for his grace; we worship him for his righteousness, and we worship him for his love. But how often do we worship him for his power?

> God is all-powerful, and God wants to be praised for his power. We worship him for his mercy; we worship him for his justice; we worship him for his grace; we worship him for his righteousness, and we worship him for his love. But how often do we worship him for his power?

---

[11] See also **Psalm 59:16; 105:4**.

Power Is the Key to the Kingdom

Note God's Word in 1 Corinthians 4:20: "For the kingdom of God does not consist in talk but in power." We Christians like to talk—a lot. We have groups that get together to talk. We have big meetings where there's a lot of talking.

If you were a time traveler in from the first century and you popped into any church in America, would you recognize it for all the talk, or would you say, "Where's the power?" I want to see some power.

Are You Experiencing God's Power?

In Philippian 4:13, Paul states, "I can do all things through him who strengthens me." The power that we can experience is not God's omnipotence but the power that he gives to us, so we can share it with others.

How do you feel right now? Do you feel powerful? Or do you feel powerless, like David in Psalm 32:4: "For day and night your hand was heavy upon me; my strength was dried up as by the heat of summer."[12]

What Kinds of Power Does God Give?

There are hundreds of verses in the Bible about God's power. Then you have all the verses about strength—strong and strengthen, which are closely related. I reviewed all these verses and decided they fit into three categories:

---

[12] See also Psalm 22:15; 31:10.

Category 1: The Unique Power of the Gospel to Change Hearts.

The first category of power that God shares with us is in his Word. It's not the gospel plus power; it's the Word plus power. It's a powerful gospel. It's a powerful Word.

Power to Testify

God's power includes giving us the power to witness. Jesus promises us power: "But you will receive power when the Holy Spirit has come upon you ... and you shall be my witnesses" (Acts 1:8). Note also, "Because our gospel came to you not only in word but also in power and in the Holy Spirit and with full conviction. You know what kind of men we proved to be among you for your sake" (1 Thessalonians 1:5).

When the power of God comes upon the person who's proclaiming the gospel, God gives the person the words to say and the opportunity to speak. Without the person's knowing what others need to hear, God knows, and then the person says it. And then later, others come to that person and say, "That was just what I needed to hear."

We should give our testimonies more often. We should give them power. What does that mean? The Word is Power. It's not our delivery that's the power. We could mumble, stutter, or speak in a soft voice or with an accent. It's not the power of the speaker; it's the power of what is spoken.

The Word Itself Is Powerful.

Another thing is going on. This first category of God's gift of power is the power of the gospel itself. People hear the Word, and the Word penetrates their stony hearts and overcomes barriers. It gets rid of stumbling blocks and clears the way for them to come to know Jesus.[13]

---

[13] See also 1 Corinthians 2:4–5.

> For Christ did not send me to baptize but to preach the gospel, and not with words of eloquent wisdom, lest the cross of Christ be emptied of its power. For the word of the cross is folly to those who are perishing, but to us who are being saved it is the power of God. (1 Corinthians 1:17–18)

The Word of God is alive. It's not dead; it's not a corpse. It's not an inanimate object. It's alive. It has its own purposes. It has its own meaning.

The Word of God is powerful. It's not powerless. It's not weak. It's not ineffectual. If you know that the Word is powerful, you can trust that the Word will do what needs to be done. It's piercing and sharp, not dull.

What does it feel like to experience the power of the Word of God?

Everyone feels something unique about the gospel's power, but here is how I felt about it. It's from a hymn by Charles Wesley:

> Long my imprisoned spirit lay,
> Fast bound by sin and nature's night.
> Thine Eye diffused a Quickening Ray.
> I woke, the dungeon flamed with light!
> My chains fell off. My heart was free.
> I rose, went forth and followed Thee.

Category 2: Everyday Sustaining Power to Endure with Patience and Joy

This power is something everyone can have. Maybe you already rely on it. Some of us need God's power just to get out of bed in the morning.

My condition means that when I wake after I've been sleeping a long time, I'm stiff and in pain until I can get my pills, and they kick in. Just getting each day started requires the power of God to be upon me. And he's there for me and provides it every day.

Observe God's words: "May you be strengthened with all power, according to his glorious might, for all endurance and patience with joy" (Colossians 1:11). That's like power to the third power, right?

What's the purpose of everyday sustaining grace? So you can endure. and make it through the day, through the week, through the year. Not just make it, but make it with patience and joy. God's power can give you a measure of patience with the impatient people that you have to deal with. And he gives you joy when sadness would be justified.

> Some of us need God's power just to get out of bed in the morning.

God's everyday sustaining power also enables you to have strength through exercise, for in Colossians 1:29, we read, "For this, I toil, struggling with all his energy that he powerfully works within me." Notice the verse does *not* say I no longer toil, no longer labor, no longer struggle, or no longer agonize. The toil and struggle continue, but you get through it, conquer it, and overcome it.

According to God's energy that he powerfully works within you, God will give you the strengths to toil, struggle, and agonize. That doesn't mean you're sick, necessarily; you might be toiling or struggling over a relationship, a financial situation, or children who have gone away from the faith. Your struggle might involve almost anything, but God is there, ready to give you the energy to powerfully work within you.

And that process is like building muscles. Sometimes his plan for your life includes trials designed to strengthen your muscles. He doesn't choose to make your situation easier; he gives you more strength.

I've experienced God's sustaining power. I shouldn't be here—I wouldn't have expected that I would be. God has healed me gradually. I'm a walking miracle. I should have been in a nursing home by now. Everyday sustaining power is something I personally experience. You can too.

This reminds me of my experience on our church's Israel

tour. I walk well on a flat surface, but it seems all of Israel is uneven ground, and I was worried about falling. Several of the men on the trip made it their personal service to hold my arms and hands when we walked on uneven ground. I was upheld by the strength of my brothers, who kept me from falling.

I wouldn't have experienced that if I was not in a situation that required it. God can bring wonderful good from any situation. What love that was. Do you want to demonstrate love? Hold others up and keep them from falling. My experience was physical, but maybe you know someone who needs to be held up spiritually. You'll have God's power to do that.

Category 3. Unusual, Extraordinary Power.

According to Acts 19:11–12, "God was performing extraordinary miracles by the hands of Paul."[14] Further Acts 5:12 states, "Now many signs and wonders were regularly done among the people by the hands of the apostles. And they were all together in Solomon's Portico."

A miracle was an extraordinary event, even in the first century. A sign is only a sign if it's unusual. Rain in Seattle—that's not a sign. It's hot in Phoenix—not a sign. It's a beautiful day in paradise here in San Diego—not a sign. A sign is something like a virgin conceiving—there's a sign for you. But when Peter healed the man lame from birth (see Acts 3:1-16) —it really happened, but just as a miracle doesn't happen every day now, it didn't happen every day then.

Extraordinary means something is not ordinary. Healings might not be ordinary, but they're still available today. God does work real miracles, instantaneously healing people. He still does it today, but most of the time the power and the miracle that we need doesn't require a violation of the laws of science.

---

[14] See also Acts 3:1–8, 2 Timothy 4:16–817.

NOTES

Chapter 13

Faith's Midlife Crisis

Be not rash with your mouth, nor let your heart be hasty to utter a word before God, for God is in heaven and you are on earth. Let your words be few. For a dream comes with much business and a fool's voice with many words. When you vow a vow to God, do not delay paying it, for he has no pleasure in fools. Pay what you vow.

—Ecclesiastes 5:1–7

Holy Ambition

When you're a little kid, the sky's the limit on what you think you can do. Someone says to a child, "What do you want to be when you grow up?" And the child might say, "An astronaut." The child's faith is unlimited.

Christian missionary and social reformer William Carey said, "Expect great things from God; attempt great things for God." That's how many of us start off. We are either young in our actual lives or young in our Christian lives, and our faith is strong.

I grew up in Texas and once took a tour of Lyndon B. Johnson's house. I thought, *People might tour my house one day. I'd better save all my homework in case historians need it*. The sky was the limit, right?

Later, as a teenager, I gave my life to the Lord. My holy

ambition, with my whole life in front of me, knew no bounds. I imagined I would be like Billy Graham in the Los Angeles Coliseum or Charles Spurgeon, speaking at the Metropolitan Tabernacle. Why not? Who's to say? Or maybe I'd find Noah's ark. (That would be pretty cool.)

However, these early days of faith adventures are often replaced by faith drudgery and the tyranny of our lifestyles. The erosion that is inflicted on us by life experiences tends to undermine our faith in a God who still has great plans for us and can do anything.

This is when the doubts creep in. Regardless of your age, it's the point in your Christian life when you plateau, or you develop a malaise.

You develop lower expectations for the future.

You stop desiring to do great things for God.

You stop expecting God to do great things for you. You kind of coast through your Christian life, thinking your Christian life will be no better than it already has been. You tell yourself, "I just need to accept that this is who I am and all I'm going to be." It's like your fuel tank reads empty.

You cease praying for the salvation of loved ones who, after many years, have never received true saving faith. You tell yourself, "He's heard the gospel over and over again for twenty years now, so if he hasn't believed by now, he never will." You didn't necessarily sit down one day and decide to cross the person off the list, but you just stopped praying for the person.

If you do offer up your friend for prayer or ask for an illness to be cured or for a sin or habit to be shaken off, you do so without any expectation that it will happen. You tell yourself, "I guess it's worth a shot. Can't hurt."

You accept an illness, weakness, or failure as permanent and inevitable. You tell yourself, "This is my cross. I better accept it." You surrender to it. You stop fighting.

You resign yourself to the presence of sin in your daily life. You tell yourself, "It's wrong, but I'm just going to be defeated fighting it, so why bother?" You quit fighting it; you stopped struggling with it.

You are single, but you date non-Christians because there just are not enough Christians you find attractive.

You are unemployed for many months, and you've not only stopped looking for a job, but you've also stopped praying for one too.

How precious did that grace appear the hour I first believed— but now, not so much.

You Don't Know All That God Is Doing

We know our God answers prayers, but sometimes after we've been Christians for a while, we become know-it-alls—we think we know everything that God is doing. The idea of putting God in a box was that the box is what you think God can do. But the real message is that God is not in your box, and he does all kinds of stuff that you don't know about or can even imagine.

Learn to trust him because of everything that he's do- ing in someone's life while you're praying for their salvation. Remember that you don't know what God is doing in another's life. Someone's sick. You don't know how God is working in that person's life. God is doing all kinds of things that you don't know about. And that's why you need to trust him.

Saying it in another way, just because we *don't* think he's do- ing something, it doesn't mean that, he's not doing it. See what it says in Ephesians 3:19: "And to know the love of Christ that surpasses knowledge, that you may be filled with all the fullness of God." So, for example, God might be working in somebody's heart that you've prayed for. God might be orchestrating all kinds of circumstances, bringing that person's life to the pinnacle of a decision. But you have no way of knowing that. You don't know what's going on with that person because you haven't checked in with him in a while. So you may think you know what God is doing with tons of stuff that you don't know about. This is always true, right? No—remember that what you know God is doing does not limit what God does.

What You Understand Does Not Limit What God Can Do

Polio legs don't get fixed; deaf ears don't suddenly hear. We tell ourselves that we understand how these things work. We think God is limited by the things that limit us. Back to the box again.

Remember the box is a construction of what limits us, and we stuff God into it. Our limits are not God's limits. Our understanding is very limited. His ways are mysterious and beyond our understanding.

> And the peace of God, which surpasses all understanding, will guard your hearts and your minds in Christ Jesus. (Philippians 4:7)

God's peace, love, mercy, and kindness are beyond our understanding. We don't know how it works. We don't know what parts are required. We don't have any assembly instructions. God is beyond all of that.

> **We think God is limited by the things that limit us. Back to the box again.**

Your Requests Do Not Restrict God's Answers

> Now in putting everything in subjection to him, he left nothing outside his control. (Hebrews 2:8b)

Our requests do not limit God's answers. We may think if we pray for something, then God must answer that request with yes or no—as if his answers are limited by what we requested.

God might give you more than you ask for. He might give you less than you ask for. He might give you something different, but what does he want? He wants you on your knees in front of him, baring your soul and bearing your problems in your heart, and he will minister to you.

> Now to him who is able to do far more abundantly than all that we ask or think, according to the power at work within us. (Ephesians 3:20)

In some modern Bible translations, the word in the above scripture that is translated as *think* is better translated as *imagine*. The "power at work within us" is the Holy Spirit. The Spirit is at work within us, enabling us to do far more than only having our prayers answered—and far more abundantly than we could ask or imagine.

> **God might give you more than you ask for. He might give you less than you ask for. He might give you something different, but what does he want? He wants you on your knees in front of him, baring your soul and bearing your problems in your heart, and he will minister to you.**

What then shall we say to these things? If God is for us, who can be against us? He who did not spare his own Son but gave him up for us all, how will he not also with him graciously give us all things? (Romans 8:31–32)

Is there a limit to what God can do for you? In the above verse, there's no limit. Even your imagination's limit is not a limit on God.

Don't Measure God by Your Experiences

I'm tempted to protest, "My left ear is deaf, and I've never seen anybody who was healed from deafness, so I don't think that's going to happen, but it's worth a shot. It can't hurt." Because we are unable, we may assume God is unable too. We think we know ourselves better than God knows us.

There's one person who knows you better than you know yourself, and that's God. He not only knows your past and your present, but he knows your future. He knows better what's good for you and what's right for you. He knows what's perfect for you, so learn from him.

In Paul's letter to the Ephesians, he writes, in Ephesians 3:1, "And God is able to make all grace abound to you, so that having all sufficiency in all things at all times, you may abound in every good work."

The love of Christ surpasses knowledge, no matter how much knowledge you have. His love is not limited by your knowledge. It's beyond your knowledge and surpasses knowledge. It's more than you can think or imagine. *Our God is greater, our God is stronger; God, you are higher than any other.*"[15] His love surpasses your knowledge now; it surpasses your knowledge later. Even in eternity, it will surpass your knowledge.

Your Unworthiness Doesn't Limit God's Grace

When you got saved, you knew that God's grace overcame your unworthiness. When you're saved, when you put your faith in Christ as he was on the cross, two things happen—well, lots of things happen, but these are two things that are for you now.

First, your sin goes on Christ, but it doesn't stop there. His perfection and righteousness are placed on you. You are clothed in Jesus's righteousness. It's not just seeing you as sin-free; your righteousness is positive through Jesus. When God sees you, he sees the righteousness of Christ. Is he seeking to hold back his mercy and kindness toward you and the righteousness of Christ? Your unworthiness does not limit God's grace. The sky is not the limit.

It says in 2 Corinthians 9:8, "And God is able to make all

---

[15] *"Our God"* lyrics by Chris Tomlin

grace abound to you, so that having all sufficiency in all things at all times, you may abound in every good work."

Wow! What a verse! You can abound in every good work because God's grace is abounding in you, giving you sufficiency in all things—always. Is there a limit to how many good works you can have? What about the subject matter of the things with which you're struggling? Is that limited? How about time? Is there a limit on the timing of the good works? This verse shows there are no limitations.

No, God promises all grace, all sufficiency, all things, all times, and every good work. That's a promise you can take to the bank.

Our weaknesses—and we have them—only reveal God's strengths. That's what they're for. You cannot rely on yourself. You must rely on God. If you have a weakness or a failure, or if your prayers are not effective, or if you still have weak faith, then come to the Savior. Come closer to him. Draw near to him.

> Three times I pleaded with the Lord about this, that it should leave me. But he said to me, My grace is sufficient for you, for my power is made perfect in weakness. Therefore, I will boast all the more gladly of my weaknesses, so that the power of Christ may rest upon me. For the sake of Christ, then, I am content with weaknesses, insults, hardships, persecutions, and calamities. For when I am weak, then I am strong. (2 Corinthians 12:8–12)

The Future Will Be Incomparable

> This momentary affliction [that's a trial you're going through, the trouble, the illness, job loss, financial struggles] is preparing you for an eternal weight of glory beyond all comparison. (2 Corinthians 4:17)

As in the words of the song, *"Nothing compares to the promise I have in you,"*[16], so Paul says similarly in 1 Corinthians 2:9: "But, as it is written, what no eye has seen, nor ear heard, nor the heart of man imagined, what God has prepared for those who love him."

His plan for you is better than any plan you could imagine. How do I know that? Because it says so in the Bible. It is not that I know it from my flesh. I know it's the Word of God and that it is trustworthy.

---

[16] *"Shout to the Lord"* lyrics by Chris Tomlin

NOTES

Chapter 14

Famous Faith Failures

Remember not the sins of my youth
or my transgressions;
according to your steadfast love remember me,
for the sake of your goodness, O Lord!

—Psalm 25:7

O Lord, rebuke me not in your anger,
nor discipline me in your wrath.
Be gracious to me, O Lord, for I am languishing;
heal me, O Lord, for my bones are troubled.
My soul also is greatly troubled.
But you, O Lord—how long?
Turn, O Lord, deliver my life;
save me for the sake of your steadfast love.

—Psalm 6:1–4

Believers and Unbelievers

Sometimes people in ordinary conversation refer to believers and unbelievers. And you might get the impression that a believer is someone who believes everything and maintains strong faith all the time. Then there are these unbelievers who don't believe in any of it. But the world is not quite like that. You cross a line when saving faith, where you put your heart in Jesus's hands; you trust him as your Lord and Savior. You rely on him only for your salvation.

But even beyond that point, Christians have different levels of strength in their faith. You might find some time, some seasons, where your faith is strong and other seasons where your faith is weak. Some people have weak faith, but what is that? One thing that characterizes weak faith is doubt. I have doubts. You likely have doubts. It's perfectly normal to have doubts, and they might appear in a wide variety of situations.

Famous Faith Failures

When you read the Bible, you will find that all the people in that Hall of Faith's famous list in Hebrews 11 had moments in their lives when their faith was weak and lacking, when they doubted either God's ability or willingness to help.

These are people to whom God talked, audibly in many cases. These are people who received a vision from God. These are people who each helped bring the Word of God—and they still lacked faith sometimes.

Moses:

Speaking to God in the burning bush:

> But Moses said to the Lord, Oh, my Lord, I am not eloquent, either in the past or since you have spoken to your servant, but I am slow of speech and of tongue. Then the Lord said to him, Who has made man's mouth? Who makes him mute, or deaf, or seeing, or blind? Is it not I, the Lord? Now therefore go, and I will be with your mouth and teach you what you shall speak. But he said, Oh, my Lord, please send someone else. (Exodus 4:1, 10, 13–14)

Moses spent forty years in the desert, waiting for God. God finally appeared to him in a burning bush. Now there was a guy out in the desert, and the bush started talking to him. It was burning, and it was talking to him. You'd think that faith would be easy at that point, right? Would you think our faith would be easy if God had burned a bush, talked to us, and told us what to do?

But even though he was talking to the bush, Moses had the audacity to say that he wouldn't be believed. "They won't listen to my voice, for they will say, The Lord did not appear to you." He then says he was not eloquent, that he was "slow in speech and of the tongue." But God said after that, "Who made your mouth?" Moses said, "Oh my Lord, please send someone else."

> Wow! The burning bush was right in front of him, and he didn't have faith that he could do what God had asked him to do.

Wow! The burning bush was right in front of him, and he didn't have faith that he could do what God had asked him to do.

He thought only of what he could do himself in his human capacity. He forgot he was talking to God.

David:

> Then David said in his heart, Now I shall perish one day by the hand of Saul. There is nothing better for me than that I should escape to the land of the Philistines. Then Saul will despair of seeking me any longer within the borders of Israel, and I shall escape out of his hand. So David arose and went over, he and the six hundred men who were with him, to Achish the son of Maoch, king of Gath. And David lived with Achish at Gath, he and his men, every man with his household, and David with his two wives, Ahinoam of Jezreel, and Abigail of Carmel, Nabal's widow. (1 Samuel 27:1–3)

Here is David. He went against Goliath and was a man of faith. He went against Goliath and said, "Why should I be afraid? I'm in the hands of the living God." Then he was chased around by Saul. Not once but twice, he captured Saul. He had Saul at his mercy, but he let Saul go twice and ran to hide with the Philistines. His faith was weak. He didn't deny the Lord; he just didn't trust the Lord.

Elijah:

> Ahab told Jezebel all that Elijah had done and how he had killed all the prophets with the sword. Then Jezebel sent a messenger to Elijah, saying, So may the gods do to me and more also, if I do not make your life as the life of one of them by this time tomorrow. Then he was afraid, and he arose and ran for his life and came to Beersheba, which belongs to Judah, and left his servant there. ... There he came to a cave and lodged in it. And behold, the word of the Lord came to him, and he said to him, What are you doing here, Elijah? He said I have been very jealous for the Lord, the God of hosts. For the people of Israel have forsaken your covenant, thrown down your altars, and killed your prophets with the sword, and I, even I only, am left, and they seek my life, to take it away. (1 Kings 19:1–3, 9–10)

And that was news to him? Where was he? This is how it's been going on for quite some time—sometimes we feel like we have weak faith. But the disciples sometimes had weak faith.

Disciples Sometimes Had Weak Faith
--Even after Miracles Were Performed before Them.

> But when he saw the wind, he was afraid, and beginning to sink he cried out, Lord, save me. Jesus immediately reached out his hand and took hold of him, saying to him, O you of little faith, why did you doubt? And when they got into the boat, the wind ceased. And those in the boat worshiped him, saying, "Truly you are the Son of God." (Matthew 14:30–32)

This beautiful story is from Peter trying to walk on the water. Peter was walking on water, and he saw the wind. Wait a minute—he was walking on water and then saw the wind, and he was afraid. It doesn't go with me somehow. He had the sequence wrong. He began to sink and cried out, "Lord save me!" That was

> They'd just fed five thousand people, but the next day they were worried about their lunch.

a good prayer. Jesus immediately reached out his hand and took Peter, saying to him, "O you of little faith, Why did you doubt?" When they got into the boat, the wind ceased.

> And they began discussing it among themselves, saying, We brought no bread. But Jesus, aware of this, said, O you of little faith, why are you discussing among yourselves the fact that you have no bread? Do you not yet perceive? Do you not remember the five loaves for the five thousand, and how many baskets you gathered? (Matthew 16:7–9)

They'd just fed five thousand people, but the next day they were worried about their lunch.

Even in the clear evidence that God does miraculous, wondrous things, sometimes we still don't believe it. This is amazing to me.

Disciples Sometimes Had Weak Faith, --Even in the Presence of the Resurrected Jesus

The disciples were startled and frightened and thought they saw a spirit. And he said to them, "As they were talking about these things, Jesus himself stood among them, and said to them, Peace to you! But they were startled and frightened and thought they saw a spirit. And he said to them, Why are you troubled, and why do doubts arise in your hearts? See my hands and my feet, that it is I myself. Touch me and see. For a spirit does not have flesh and bones as you see that I have. And when he had said this, he showed them his hands and his feet. And while they still disbelieved for joy and were marveling, he said to them, Have you anything here to eat? They gave him a piece of broiled fish, and he took it and ate before them. (Luke 24:37–39)

And in Matthew 28:16–17, it says, "Now the eleven disciples went to Galilee, to the mountain to which Jesus had directed them. And when they saw him, they worshiped him, but some doubted." The disciples were in the physical, visible, and touchable presence of the resurrected Savior. This was after he rose.

Isn't that amazing? They'd already seen the resurrected Jesus in Jerusalem. He came to the upper room, and Thomas touched him. Later, they were in Galilee, and still some doubted. That means *more than one* of them doubted in the presence of the resurrected Savior. Is that amazing? That is a weak faith.

How Should We Treat Those with Weak Faith?

- Welcome them (Romans 14:1).
- Bear with them. "We who are strong have an obligation to bear with the failings of the weak, and not to please ourselves" (Romans 15:1).

- Don't dismiss them as unbelievers. Counsel them. Bear with the failings of the weak. Don't judge them. Don't condemn them. Help them. Pray for them.
- Have mercy on them (Jude 1:21–2).

Paul wouldn't have written Romans 14:1 or Romans 15:1, if there weren't people in the church who had weak faith. Accordingly, there must be a bunch of people in our churches who have doubts.

NOTES

Chapter 15

Dealing with Doubts

Mark 9 is about a sick boy's devoted but doubting dad—a dad with doubts and weak faith. This chapter really spoke to me because it's a story—on the surface—about a boy who's sick whom Jesus heals. But just below the surface is a powerful story about his dad. His dad loved him, took care of him, and did whatever was required, but he had doubts and weak faith.

This story isn't only for the person with a strong faith or weak faith. It's especially for the following kinds of people: parents of a handicapped child, parents of an autistic child, parents of a Down syndrome child, the spouse or another caregiver of someone with a chronic illness. Notice I said a *spouse or another caregiver* because this is a story more about the dad as the caregiver, than it is about the boy.

> And he asked them, What are you arguing about with them? And someone from the crowd answered him, Teacher, I brought my son to you, for he has a spirit that makes him mute. And whenever it seizes him, it throws him down, and he foams and grinds his teeth and becomes rigid. So I asked your [Jesus's] disciples to cast it out, and they were not able. (Mark 9:16–18)

Mark's story starts out when Jesus came down from the mountain of transfiguration. He revealed he was the Son of God with his radiant glory, visible to Peter, James, and John. When Jesus met with the rest of the disciples, they saw a great crowd around them, and the scribes were arguing with them. As soon as the crowd saw Jesus, they ran up to him and greeted him. Jesus then asked what the argument was about but got an answer from someone who had not been asked. And he answered them, "O faithless generation, how long am I to be with you? How long am I to bear with you?" (Mark 9:19)

In Mark 9:22b–24, Jesus was somewhat frustrated. Jesus later said, in godly frustration, that he expected the disciples to pray to him and to ask him to be healed, and they didn't do that. They tried to do it with their own power, and Jesus was frustrated with that.

Now that we can see the context of the dad's admittedly weak assertion of faith—"Jesus, if you can do anything, have compassion on us and help us"—maybe we can cut the poor guy some slack. After all, the disciples had failed to heal the boy. Dad had nothing but bad news for years. He was hanging on by a thread.

The spirit did it right there in front of Jesus, in front of the entire crowd. The spirit thought he was a victor at that point. After all, the disciples had failed to heal him, and Dad had doubts.

How Much Dad Loved His Son.

Remember the crowd was running to Jesus. Imagine a crowd running, and you're trying to get to Jesus too. And you're bringing the boy with you.

Did the dad drag the boy past

> Did the dad drag the boy past the fires? Or did he carry the boy on his shoulders? Or maybe put the boy in a cart or small wagon. To keep up with the crowd, he must have been running too. How did that work? A crowd of people was competing for Jesus's attention.

the fires? Or did he carry the boy on his shoulders? Or maybe put the boy in a cart or small wagon. To keep up with the crowd, he must have been running too. How did that work? A crowd of people was competing for Jesus's attention.

And this dad made it all the way to Jesus. Somehow, he fought to get to Jesus through a running crowd and got to the front.

Luke's account states that then the dad fell on his knees. We know from Luke that the boy was his only son, his only child. This man would do anything for his only child. He was completely devoted to his loved one who was sick.

Dad Must Have Had Many Doubts

Imagine that the dad tried to go to the synagogue for years. "Oh, that's the guy with the demon kid." I'll bet it was brutal for him to even walk through town to buy groceries. Whose fault was it?

The dad must have wondered, "Why, Lord? Why is this afflicting my son? Why would a demon afflict my son? Why?" He must have gone over and over this question in his mind. Why did this happen? Why, Lord? Why?

John 9 lets us know what the world was like back then. People would assume that if your child was sick, it was the child's fault or the parents' fault. The only way they understood suffering was that somehow God was punishing people.

Let's take a short trip to John 9.

> As he passed by, he saw a man blind from birth. And his disciples asked him, Rabbi, who sinned, this man or his parents, that he was born blind? Jesus answered, It was not that this man sinned, or his parents, but that the works of God might be displayed in him. (John 9:1–3)

But what about the dad? He had been taking care of his only son for many years. Pagan medicine men couldn't heal the boy.

The rabbis couldn't heal him. Temple sacrifices couldn't heal him. Prayers by the elders didn't heal him. Even Jesus's disciples were unable to get rid of the demon.

What must it have been like for all those years? Feel for Dad as he waited and waited. All hope must have nearly left him. His love for his son never left, but his hope for healing probably nearly left him. With each day, it must have seemed less and less likely that his son would be healed.

How Exhausted the Dad Must Have Been

Jesus asked the dad, "How long has this been happening to him?"

And the dad answered, "From childhood. And it has often cast him into the fire and into the water to destroy him."

Remember this child couldn't talk. In the years of raising his only son, the father never heard, "I love you, Daddy." He never heard, "Thank you, Daddy." Just silence all those years.

When my older boy was a baby, and we put him in a car seat, he would say something like this as we drove around: "Mommy, Mommy, Mommy, Mommy, Mommy." And my wife would say, "What, Alex?" And Alex would say, "Love you." Every now and then, he said it to Daddy too, but mostly it was Mommy.

This dad never heard that, but it didn't stop him from loving his son to the point of sacrifice. How much the dad loved his son is evidenced by his willingness to take his son away from the safety of the home.

Remember the illness this boy had—he'd fall on the ground and had bruises, cuts, or even concussions and burns because the devil had tried to throw him into the fire. There would have been open fires in various places in villages at that time.

Think about what he had to do to take his son from the safety of his home. This boy probably had lived in the house his entire life. He didn't go out for regular excursions; it would've been too dangerous—fighting a running crowd, facing embarrassment and ridicule.

The story goes on.

> And it has often cast him into the fire and into the water, to destroy him. But if you can do anything, have compassion on us and help us. Jesus said to him, "if you can?" "Immediately the father of the child cried out and said, "I believe, help my unbelief." And Jesus said to him—" If you can! All things are possible for one who believes. (Mark 9:22–29)

You're talking to me "if I can"? Jesus says, "All things are possible for one who believes." Jesus can do anything for anyone who believes. I love this.

And when Jesus saw that a crowd came running together, he rebuked the unclean spirit, saying to it, You mute and deaf spirit, I command you, come out of him and never enter him again. And after crying out and convulsing him terribly, it came out, and the boy was like a corpse so that most of them said, He is dead. But Jesus took him by the hand and lifted him up, and he arose. And when he had entered the house, his disciples asked him privately, Why could we not cast it out? And he said to them," This kind cannot be driven out by anything but prayer."(Mark 9:25-29)

This is such a short but profound statement. It's one that many of us, including me, identify with. But what did it mean, and how can we understand this? I would like to make some observations:

The Dad Didn't Make His Belief Conditional

God's promises to his people are unconditional. God's graces are unconditional. God's love for you is unconditional.

How often do we look at God to make our faith and our love of him conditional? Our love for God and our faith and trust in God needs to be unconditional. Unconditional means you trust God for whatever circumstances you're in—unconditionally.

You love God because he saved you. You love God because he is God. Praise God; he saved you. But you certainly don't make your love conditional upon what he does because he has a plan for you greater than you can imagine. His plan is far better than what you would require of him. And who are you to put conditions on God?

His Doubts Were Not Prerequisites

People all around the father and son probably were saying, "Why would you expect every child to get healed?" People would've told him to quit and stop expecting it, but he didn't stop. He took his doubts, and he threw them to the feet of Jesus.

He did not say, "Lord, I believe for the most part, but I have a few questions to ask you first."

He didn't make Jesus solve all his doubts and questions first and then accept Jesus. He just trusted God and said, "God, I have these problems. I have these doubts. I have these weaknesses. Help me with them." He turned them over to Jesus and trusted Jesus to fix them.

Jesus Did Not Require Stronger Faith

Jesus did not say, "If you get no miracle, it's your fault because you lack enough faith." He looked right into the eye of the dad and said that even he could have a miracle.

Jesus Did Not Make His Miracle Conditional

Even those who have weak faith can get a miracle. Amen? Jesus did not say if you have faith, you can do anything. That's because it's God who does the miracles.

The Dad Took Responsibility for His Unbelief

He didn't say, "Lord, I believe; help my son." There is no doubt that he wanted his son to be healed, but he said, "Lord, I believe.

Help my unbelief." Whether it was his fault or not doesn't matter. He took responsibility for his unbelief. And he basically asked God to do two healings here—heal his son, and heal him of his unbelief. *I'm afflicted with unbelief. Heal me too.* Notice that he didn't make his faith contingent.

He understood at that point that Jesus was Lord—able to heal—and Savior—willing to heal. The result was he placed all his trust in Jesus, who was able and willing to heal.

The last part of the story almost seems anticlimactic to me.

> But Jesus took him by the hand and lifted him up,
> and he arose. (Mark 9:27)

That's a great ending to any story. That's a powerful miracle, but to me, it serves as anticlimax because I think the story is about the dad.

It is about the boy too, of course, but it's really about the dad and all the other dads out there—the dads who fought to get to the front of the crowd; the dad who suffered from seeing the disciples fail to heal his son; the dad who suffered for years in taking care of the child who was housebound; the dad who had no logical human reason for hope but put his faith in Jesus. He went from being an unbeliever to a believer. Or maybe from being someone with little faith to someone with strong faith during the course of this conversation. That's a miracle, isn't it?

You don't have to figure out all the answers to your doubts. You just must trust Jesus Christ and put your trust and your life in his hands. He will solve those problems. He will answer those questions. He will deal with those doubts. You can come, as this man did. You can come to the Lord and say, "Lord, I trust you. I have all this baggage, and we need to work on that. I have baggage, Lord, but I trust you, and I love you."

NOTES

Chapter 16

Thank God for Everything

Offer to God a sacrifice of thanksgiving,
and perform your vows to the Most High,
and call upon me in the day of trouble;
I will deliver you, and you shall glorify me.

—Psalm 50:14–15

Give thanks in all circumstances; for this is the will
of God in Christ Jesus for you.

—1 Thessalonians 5:18

German Manners

When our children were young (they are adults now), we had girls from Europe called *au pairs* living in our home to assist with the children.

The girls had proper visas that were obtained from a US government–approved agency. There were lots of rules designed to benefit both the au pair and the host family.

One girl was from Germany. My wife told me I needed to speak to her because my wife would prepare and cook the dinner for the whole family, but this girl never said thank you.

I didn't waste any time. I said, "I need to speak to you about saying thank you to Justine when she prepares and serves you dinner."

The girl gave me a blank stare, taking a few minutes to answer. Finally, she said, "I shouldn't have to thank you because according to the au pair rules and guidelines, the host family is required to feed the au pair."

This left me dumbfounded. What were German moms and dads teaching their children? Was this a cultural thing or just a rude young lady?

She didn't feel grateful, so she didn't say thank you. She wasn't grateful because, in her eyes, we were only doing what we had to do. She didn't thank us for fulfilling obligations. She didn't see the need to thank someone for doing something the person was required to do. It reminded me of the miser who only tipped when the person went over and above what was required

> She didn't see the need to thank someone for doing something the person was required to do.

This sounds logical, but it is not. If we lived in this girl's world, we wouldn't thank the veteran for his service, we wouldn't thank the first responder for saving our baby, and we wouldn't thank the postman for delivering our mail. They were just doing their jobs. They were doing something that was required of them.

I think I came to a better understanding of why God wants to be thanked and why we like to thank him. Everything we are and have is owed to God, and everything we receive from him is a gracious gift, unearned and unrequired. God, in his kindness and mercy, bestows benefits and gifts to us all.

As a result, even though we are commanded in the scriptures to thank God in numerous sets of circumstances, we don't thank God because we are required to; we thank him because we are grateful.

And the more we thank him, the more grateful we become.

> We don't thank God because we are required to; we thank him because we are grateful.

Why We Thank Him

The German girl thought good things were her entitlement, her right. Remember when I said that in today's world, many believe they have a right to be happy?

Thank God for His Gracious Gifts

Paul writes in 2 Corinthians 9:15, "Thanks be to God for his inexpressible gift." He means you should thank God for showing mercy and undeserved kindness to you. Thank God for his plan for your life, which is better than you can imagine.

God-given joy is not our right; it is a gift of God and one for which we are grateful and hence want to thank God, commandment or no commandment.

In Psalm 107:21, 31, it says, "Let them thank the Lord for his steadfast love, for his wondrous works to the children of man!" I will share two observations on what is said here: first, we must look upon our lives as full of examples, illustrations, and meanings, in each case reflecting the marvelous working out of our lives by God and in accordance with his plan. Second, as we remember what God has already done in our lives, we acknowledge and thank God for his having done so, even while we go back to the well and ask him to do it again. But never must we act as though we would say to God, "What have you done for me lately?"

The Thanksgiving Circle

My family has experimented a lot with the celebration of Thanksgiving and Christmas. One year we had about a dozen people to the house, and we formed a big circle, holding hands. I had given advance notice that before dinner, we would go around the room, and each person would mention something for which he or she was thankful. Although everyone had at least two hours to identify something for which they were thankful, I was very disappointed with the results.

As we went around the big circle, I heard, "Uh, thank you, God, for my health." And "Thank you for Justine, who cooked this food," and "Thanks for family," and "Thanks for the good weather for those who were traveling."

I too am grateful for my health, even with Parkinson's. I am also grateful for family and good weather. And last but definitely not least, I certainly remembered to thank my wife for making the feast we would soon enjoy. Still, I wondered, *Is this the best they can come up with?* Were they so awash in a feeling of entitlement that they failed to see the countless gifts they received?

We must remind our children to say thank you so that they will be appreciative of their many blessings. In the same way, God wants us to say thank you so that we will be appreciative. It is not that he needs to hear it; it's that we need to say it—out loud. We have been commanded to be grateful and to express our thankfulness to God as a way of teaching us, rather than having us recite insincere flattery.

Thank God for Saving You Every Day

Psalm 118:21 tells us, "I thank you that you have answered me and have become my salvation." David describes thanking God as his "salvation" or "deliverer." He uses *deliverer* and *salvation*, meaning that God was, is, and continues to be the one who delivers David at all times and in all respects. He doesn't thank God for having delivered him in the past and from God's wrath but for delivering him from sin and danger every single day. A deliverer always delivers, and he delivers from all dangers.

To clarify, when Paul writes in 1 Corinthians 1:4 that we should thank God for the Corinthians "because of the grace of God that was given to" them, he is making it clear that it is *grace* that saves us—through faith, to be sure, but he thanks God for the salvation of the Corinthians. He is not thanking the Corinthians.

Salvation in the New Testament is not merely about that one day in the past when you were saved. It's about being saved continually throughout your life. Let us feel the need to be saved each and every day, regardless of any calendar date we identify as the day we were born again.

Let us not merely thank God for having saved us one day in the past; let us thank God for saving us each day as it comes. Let us thank God for saving us tomorrow because we know that even tomorrow, we will once again fall short. It is our nature.

Thank God for Not Giving Up on You

Psalms 107:1 says, "Oh give thanks to the Lord, for he is good, for his steadfast love endures forever!"[17]

Through all the experiences I've described above, I understand now—better than I ever could have previously—that it is truly God who perseveres, even when we do not. His love is unfailing. If he left it up to us, we'd all rebel against God, resist him, and suffer eternal separation from him. It's our nature. But God's grace overtakes us with his unfailing love. And that's good. Take it from me; that's very, very good.

Thank God Because You Love Him

More than a decade ago, I was driving my then-four-year-old daughter, Mallory, home from preschool. The doting father that I am, I thought she was the perfect child. She seemed to behave so well, both at home and away. On this day, the teacher had gone out of her way to tell me how much she liked Mallory. As I looked in my rearview mirror at the little girl in the back seat, we had the following short conversation:

> Dad: Mallory, you were so good today. I am so proud of you. You are such a good girl.

---

[17] See also Psalm 118:1; 29; 136:3, 26; 1 Chronicles 16:3.

Mallory: I know that.
Dad: Mallory, why are you such a good girl?
Mallory: Because I love you.
Dad: You're good because you love me?
Mallory: Yeah.

Thinking about these verses in the context of my conversation with Mallory made me wonder—had I misunderstood the connection between love and obedience? I was very familiar with the verses that seemed to say that I'd prove my love by my obedience, but had I misunderstood them until now?

I confess I'd heard myself saying to my own kids, sometimes in the fit of anger after their misbehavior, "If you love me, why do you disobey me?" I would try to make them feel guiltier by saying, "If you loved me, you wouldn't have done that."

Is that what Jesus was saying? Was he telling us to obey more to prove our love, or was he telling us to love him more in order that we might obey?

I think I've been reading those verses all wrong. Jesus wasn't saying that by our obedience, we can prove that we love him or that by our disobedience we prove that we don't, even though such behavior is, in fact, proof.

I believe he was saying that our love for him will bring forth the fruit of obedience, and if we do not have that love, we will not have the fruit.

It seems this is true. Romans 1:5 says, "Through whom we have received grace and apostleship to bring about the obedience of faith for the sake of his name among all the nations," establishing that there is a form of obedience that is the pure fruit of the Holy Spirit and that constitutes effective evidence of the Holy Spirit's work in our lives. I believe faith and obedience have a cause-and-effect relationship.

The direct link had been lost on me but not on my daughter, who seemed to understand this intuitively and without a doubt.

Love God and increase your love for him, and the fruit will be obedience to his commands; that is, greater righteousness.

Thank God for Everything, Even Parkinson's Disease

> Give thanks in all circumstances; for this is the will of God in Christ Jesus for you. (1 Thessalonians 5:18)

We must view the above scripture in two ways: First, it thanks God for the collective entirety of our lives, with the emphasis on the universality of our thanks. And second, it thanks him for each individual thing God has done in our lives.

I'm reminded of a certain concept in the way we view scripture. We believe in what is called the *verbal, plenary inspiration* of scripture. That means we believe the entire Bible is God's Word (hence, *plenary*), and we also believe each individual word of the Bible is God's Word (hence, *verbal*). A similar concept should apply to our thanksgiving. We thank him for the whole of our lives, and we thank him for each individual part.

In my case, that means I thank him for my Parkinson's. You will need to develop an attitude of thankfulness for yourself, even for the pain and hardship you endure (for all the reasons stated in this book). And don't just thank him for being our Savior. That shows no faith or trust. Anyone can thank God for something positive they've received—a job promotion, for example, or being healed. We need to be thankful for the disease, trial, or tribulation while we are still experiencing it.

So how should we thank him?

Thank Him Like You're Not Embarrassed

David made his private accounts with God into public accounts. We should all be certified public accountants within our relationships with God. Psalm 18:49a says your thanks is to be made in front of the entire nation, and Psalms 100:4 uses the very public phrase, "Enter his gates with thanksgiving and his courts with praise!"

The gates of an ancient Jewish town were where the town's

elders met to discuss public matters. His courts were the courts of the temple. There was absolutely nothing secret, hidden, or private about the temple's sacrificial system in the Old Testament. Worship was an entirely public affair. And so should your thanksgiving be.

Thank Him Like You Really Mean It

In Hebrew as well as in English, a thanksgiving that is sincere may be described as being "from the heart." The phrase in both languages also is used to mean *with love and affection.*

Accordingly, in Psalms 30: 2, David sings praises to God: "O Lord my God, I cried to you for help, and you have healed me." Your prayer and your singing should, in all cases, be sincere and with love and affection for God.

Gallery

Randy at age six.

At age eight with Tom and Randy's mother (1969)

Randy at age 20, in Greece.

Randy trying to blend into Rome, Italy, Fall of 1981.

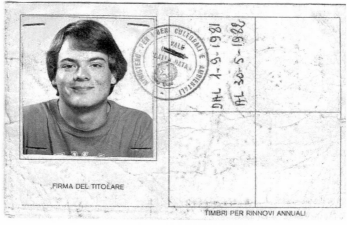

Caption: Randy's life saving museum pass.

Randy at the Republican National Convention in Dallas, summer 1984.

Randy at the time he became a member of the Texas Bar, 1989

Randy at the time of diagnosis, 1999

Randy, twenty years after diagnosis

Postscript

As of this writing, it has been twenty years since I was diagnosed. By all accounts, I'm doing very well. To ensure that I could keep working, I kept my Parkinson's secret for the ten years following my diagnosis. At age forty-nine, I finally retired early from my job as an attorney, but I'm enjoying my time in ministry.

Appendix

Prayer for a Friend Who Is Ill

It is always preferable to pray with people in person, but in our modern society, friends often are far away. Frequently, the only communication is email. How can you pray for someone in an email? In such a circumstance, it can be effective and even powerful—God willing—to write out your prayer and send it to your friend so that he or she knows exactly what you prayed.

Below is an example of such a prayer that I sent to someone very far away, yet very dear to my heart.

> Our heavenly Father,
>
> I lift before you my dear friend, who has been told she has cancer and will have surgery. I ask that you hear my prayers on her behalf and that you grant my requests in the name of Jesus.
>
> Father, I ask that you relieve her of any pain or suffering she may presently be experiencing.
>
> I pray that you give her peace of mind, courage, and relief from anxiety that certainly must be facing her.
>
> If there is even the tiniest shadow of a doubt in her mind about her total assurance of salvation through your Son Jesus Christ's death through the cross, please cast all such doubts away, and

grant her total and complete faith in you—faith that springs forth unto eternal life.

Please give her doctors the utmost skill, knowledge, care, and consideration for her leading up to the surgery, during the surgery, and during recovery.

I pray that your divine guidance will prevent any errors of knowledge or judgment, that your divine hand will prevent any mistakes during the procedures, and that the procedures will be successful and complete.

I also pray for her entire family. I ask that you give them all faith and comfort to endure this trial with her and that you give them wisdom and patience to help her prepare for and undergo this trial.

Father, I recognize that sometimes your will is beyond our finding out and that sometimes you have better things in mind for your children, which we may not know or even understand. However, I trust your promise that all things will work together for good for those who love God and are called according to your purpose.

About the Author

Randy Broberg is a lay pastor at Maranatha Chapel, a Calvary Chapel congregation, located in San Diego, California, with more than five thousand in weekly attendance. At Maranatha, Randy has served as an instructor in the School of Ministry, as a professor in the Maranatha Bible College, as a member of the elder and deacon board, and as a lay pastor.

Prior to the last eight years in Christian ministry, Randy was an attorney with more than twenty-five years of experience advising corporations and negotiating agreements related to their intellectual property and technology.

Before Randy retired from the practice of law to work in Christian ministry, he was awarded the title of Super Lawyer five years in a row and also the title of Top Attorney three times. Martindale-Hubbell, an information services company to the legal professions, granted him five out of five stars, based on peer review. Randy was identified in several publications as one of the top intellectual property attorneys in the country.

In early 1997, the San Diego County Superior Court appointed him to advise the court on intellectual property in connection with the mass suicide of the Heaven's Gate cult members.

Randy served five years as a legislative assistant for the US House of Representatives. His most notable congressional achievements were amending the US tax code to deny foreign tax credits for taxes paid to countries that sponsor terrorism, and renaming the street where the US Holocaust Memorial Museum is located from Fifteenth Street SW to Raoul Wallenberg Place, after the Swedish diplomat who saved more than one hundred thousand Jews from the Nazi death camps.

Randy has been a guest on *San Diego Entrepreneurship* talk radio fifteen times and has also appeared on television (Fox News and CNBC) and Radio (NPR--National Public Radio), and CNBC. He has been quoted as an expert on intellectual property by the Associated Press, the *New York Times*, *USA Today*, *Fox News*, *PC Magazine*, *ABC News*, *Investor's Business Daily*, *ComputerWorld*, *Advertising Age*, and the *Wall Street Journal*.

Since 1997, Randy has been an instructor of several intellectual property courses at the University of California, San Diego.

Randy earned his JD in 1989 from the University of Virginia School of Law, where he was a senior editor of the *Virginia Journal of Law and Politics*. In 1983, Randy received his BA in both history and classics from Stanford University. At Stanford, Randy was inducted into the academic honor society, Phi Beta Kappa, and served the *Stanford Daily* as a news reporter, a weekly bylined op-ed columnist, and as a member of the newspaper's editorial board.

In 1981, Randy also attended the American School of Classical Studies in Athens, Greece, and the Intercollegiate Center for Classical Studies in Rome, Italy.'

In 1985, Randy was a participant of a congressional mission to Santiago, Chile to review of progress being made toward the democratization of Chile after the death of its dictator, General Pinochet.

Randy spent the summer of 1986 in Degeberga, Sweden, as a farm hand and as a shepherd of sheep and goats, but currently resides in San Diego with his wife of 30 years and counting, Justine.